Monsters
of the Pacific
Northwest

Dedication:
To those who are brave enough to talk about the things that they see, feel, and experience—running the risk that others might think they're lying. We believe you.

Content Warning: This book contains retellings of historical events. Some include references to suicide, murder, and cannibalism and may not be appropriate for all audiences.

Cover design by Jonathan Norberg
Text design by Karla Linder
Edited by Ryan Jacobson and Jenna Barron
Proofread by Emily Beaumont

All images copyrighted.
Shelley Anderson: 126; **Brianna Royle Koqka:** 127
ADK branding background by **chyworks/Shutterstock.com**
Images used under license from Shutterstock.com:
Covers and silhouettes: **Sergey Arkhipov:** sasquatch;
RAYYARTS: owl
Interior: **JM-MEDIA:** 1; **Joeprachatree:** 69

10 9 8 7 6 5 4 3 2 1

Monsters of the Pacific Northwest: Stories about Bigfoot, Sea Serpents, and Other Legendary Creatures
Copyright © 2025 by Jessica Freeburg and Natalie Fowler
Published by Adventure Publications
An imprint of AdventureKEEN
310 Garfield Street South
Cambridge, Minnesota 55008
(800) 678-7006
www.adventurepublications.net
All rights reserved
Printed in the USA
Cataloging-in-Publication data is available from
the Library of Congress.
ISBN 978-1-64755-472-9 (pbk.); 978-1-64755-473-6 (ebook)

Monsters
of the
Pacific
Northwest

Jessica Freeburg & Natalie Fowler

Table of Contents

Acknowledgments

To those who have shared their stories throughout the years, even if we didn't include them here, thank you. Especially when what you were sharing seemed strange and unbelievable, you were brave to tell us. We wouldn't be able to create these books without your courage.

Important Note

Curiosity sometimes leads people to go out looking for ghosts and monsters, but please respect the law, as well as the rights and privacy of others.

Most importantly, we ask anyone who investigates the paranormal to exhibit extreme caution. Do not take this lightly. Tragically, people have died while pursuing legends. Your life is precious, and it is not worth risking. If there is any danger, please, let the legends remain as legends.

Furthermore, the information provided in this book is for reading entertainment purposes only. The authors and publisher do not assume and hereby disclaim any liability to any party for any loss, damage, or disruption caused by any other use of this information.

Preface

Legends are stories that have been handed down through the generations. One must remember that, sometimes, these retellings are like playing a marathon game of "telephone."

We authors are researchers of the paranormal. We do so with curiosity but also with an appreciation for evidence. While we strive to keep an open mind, we never turn off our logical brains. The primary-source documentation, which served as the foundation of each story chosen for this book, is critical for our purposes.

The stories reflect extensive and thorough research about some of the most well-known and notorious monster sightings and legends ever reported in the Pacific Northwest, even going back several centuries. Using evidence gathered through eyewitness interviews, newspaper articles, and other published accounts, we stay true to the facts while adapting a narrative style to recreate these encounters in a more entertaining fashion for our readers.

When recounting monster legends, it's important to acknowledge that the study of cryptozoology and the search for unknown creatures are what help us identify new classifications of animals that we never knew existed. For example, in this book, we share a story centered on the giant Pacific octopus. It is the largest of all 300 types of octopus species and was only discovered in 1910. The truth is that sometimes the things we think of as "monsters" are simply species waiting to be identified.

It is also important to remember that not everything you read on the Internet is true. Take, for example, the Pacific Northwest tree octopus. An allegedly endangered species, it was said to live both on land (in trees) and in the water. It didn't take long to realize its very existence was a complete fabrication. Its website was created in 1998 as a hoax by Lyle Zapato. It was intended to test students' and readers' ability to discern fake news. Most failed to do so. The case is still used as a classroom example on Internet literacy.

Likewise, while personal experiences that get reported in the news or other sources cannot always be substantiated, we must remember that, oftentimes, the person sharing their story faces ridicule, judgment, and disbelief. The idea that a monstrous beast is lurking in our favorite forest or within the depths of a popular river or lake is often too much to take.

This is why we are both deeply grateful for the eyewitnesses who found the courage to share their sightings. We hope their bravery might inspire others to share their stories too. When there are multiple sightings of the same creature, it adds credibility to the account.

So shut off the lights and snuggle in with your flashlight to read about some of the most terrifying and exciting monsters that have been sighted in the Pacific Northwest. Never mind that throaty growl you hear coming from behind the bushes. It's probably just a bear passing through.

—Jessica Freeburg and Natalie Fowler

Monster Creatures of the Land & Sky

Bigfoot of the Cascades
Cascade Mountains, Oregon
1997

Jess had been hiking uphill for a couple of hours. Sunlight peeked through the canopy of trees above, the forest floor speckled by rays of light filtering through the leaves. It was an especially nice day, and after a full shift of work as a deputy sheriff, Jess was happy to spend time alone in nature, taking in the beauty of the Cascade Mountains. He still had 2 hours before the sun would set. He planned to make the most of it.

He'd moved to the region when his friend, the local sheriff, offered him a job. As a former marine, Jess's life's work was serving and protecting others. He was happy to be in a new role, in a new place, that allowed him to continue doing that.

This area of the mountainside was particularly remote. With the rocky terrain stretching 260 miles across and 90 miles wide, Jess imagined there were areas around him that had yet to be explored by humans. People had only touched the edges of the remote volcanic mountain range that stretches from northern California all the way to the center of British Columbia.

As Jess ventured off the main trails, he found himself in a thicket of trees and decided to look for a more open area. He checked his map and estimated roughly where he was, then took out his compass to get his bearings.

Movement on a nearby ridge caught his eye. Someone—or rather, *something*—was watching him. It was a human-like beast, standing on two legs and covered in thick, dark fur.

What is that? Jess wondered, cocking his head to one side.

The creature cocked its head in response, mimicking Jess's exact movement.

Jess's breath caught in his throat as he realized that it was observing him, just as he was observing it.

Instinctively, Jess reached for the gun in his holster. The creature seemed to know exactly what Jess was doing, even before the gun was drawn. It darted away at super-human speed.

Curiosity won the battle between playing it safe and searching for answers. Jess rushed toward the ridge and found himself looking over an open area. His eyes scanned his surroundings, but he saw no sign of the beast. Jess surveyed the ground, looking for tracks, but found nothing. It was as if the beast had disappeared, just like a puff of smoke would evaporate in the breeze.

He continued searching. While he found no sign of the bipedal animal, he couldn't shake the anxious knot that had formed in his stomach. His inner voice screamed in his head to get out of there.

Gazing at the position of the sun, Jess realized that if he didn't start making his way back to his vehicle, he wouldn't get there before nightfall. The thought of being in the woods with that thing after dark—without a flashlight—caused a shiver to run up his spine. He shifted course and began his descent.

As he gazed to his left—in the direction the creature had run—he heard a colossal crack in the thicket to his right. It was as if a tree had broken in half.

Goose bumps raised on his arms, as Jess realized the creature had circled back to him. He heard another snap, like branches breaking. His heartbeat quickened as the truth set in: He was no longer the hunter, searching for answers. He was the prey.

He broke into a run.

As he rushed down the hill, he stopped abruptly. A deer was standing directly in his path. Jess was transfixed. The deer glanced at him casually, oddly undisturbed by his sudden presence.

The sun was falling below the treeline. Time was precious, and this deer needed to get out of Jess's way. The deer raised its head and sniffed the air as it looked behind Jess. Its body stiffened before it turned and dashed in the other direction.

The deer had sensed the thing chasing Jess, and it was terrified.

That is not a good sign, Jess thought.

He hurried onward. His boots pounded against the underbrush, dust rising in his wake. The muscles in his legs burned and his lungs ached, but fear-fueled adrenaline pushed him forward.

He broke into a sprint, knowing his vehicle was just minutes away. When the car was within sight, he realized that the sound of twigs snapping behind him were less frequent. The beast seemed to be slowing its pace.

The thought did little to calm Jess. He pulled his keys from his pocket and pressed the unlock button as he raced toward the car. He swung the door open, leapt inside, and slammed the door shut behind him.

Jess jammed the key into the ignition and twisted it—but nothing happened.

"Come on!" Jess yelled, trying again.

Nothing.

He glanced toward the woods, afraid the creature would pounce on the car at any second.

"Please, start," he pleaded, turning the keys again.

The engine puttered to life.

Simultaneously pressing the gas and shifting the gear into drive, Jess tore away from the side of the road.

His breathing returned to normal, and his heartbeat slowed. Jess didn't know what to make of his experience. He couldn't say for certain what the creature was, but he knew it was like nothing he'd ever seen before.

In the days that followed, he was hesitant to say anything about the encounter. But ultimately, he needed to share his experience. He knew the sheriff well, and he decided to trust him.

"You're never going to believe what happened out on the mountain," Jess started. The story poured out. "You probably think I've lost my mind," he ended.

"I sure don't," the sheriff replied. "Reports of an unknown beast in the mountains are pretty common around here. That said, I suggest we keep this experience between us. There's no need to file a report and get people riled up."

Jess nodded. He was relieved but not comforted. If so many others had reported seeing the creature, it could mean more than one of them were hiding in the woods, watching.

As he traveled the highways during his shifts in the coming days, he felt a sense of dread. What would the creature have done if it caught him? Would he have made it out of the forest, or would he have become another lost hiker?

One thing he knew for certain: His days of hiking the remote terrain of the Cascade Mountains were done. If that territory belonged to the creature, Jess would stick to civilization and let him have it.

Colville Sasquatch

Colville, Washington
March 19, 2024

"**S**tevens County Sheriff's Office, how can I direct your call?" Ruby doodled on a piece of paper as she stifled a yawn.

"Yeah, hello," a man's voice crackled across the line. "I am coming to the Big Meadow Lake area in mid-April to do some squatchin'."

Colville had been a Bigfoot hotspot since 1971, when giant footprints were found in the grain fields at a community dump not far from town. Newspapers across the country ran the story. The feet left impressions that were 16 inches long with a stride estimated to be over 4 feet. Six professional hunters later spent a year searching for the creature responsible for those prints.

"Squatching?" Ruby asked. She was well aware of the term. She just wasn't sure why anyone hunting for Bigfoot would call the sheriff's office.

He replied, "I want to make sure I'm following the laws. I've done some research, but the state laws about Bigfoot hunting are unclear."

"You might want to call Fish and Wildlife for that."

"I already called them," he replied. "They told me to call you."

"I see," Ruby replied. "I can get a message to our deputies for you."

"Great, thank you," the man replied, clearly relieved to be making progress. "I need to know two things. First, is it legal to shoot a sasquatch in Stevens County? And if so, do I just need a regular hunting license for that? Of course, I won't shoot any females."

"I'll pass along your questions," Ruby replied, keeping her tone professional despite an inclination to laugh.

"I want to do this right, so if someone doesn't reach out today, I'll call back tomorrow," the man said before ending the call.

* * *

Jake scrolled through his phone messages while waiting for the waitress to bring his food to the table. Ajay returned from the bathroom and sat across from him.

"Check this out," Jake said. "The sheriff's office posted on social media that some guy asked them if he needed a hunting license to hunt Bigfoot."

Ajay leaned forward. "What'd they say?"

"It doesn't look like they really answered the question."

"We're only armed with cameras, so I guess it doesn't matter to us," Ajay replied.

"The patrol chief called the guy back and told him there aren't any Sasquatch in Stevens County because one of his deputies would have accidentally hit one with a patrol car by now."

The waitress set their orders on the table. The smell of cheeseburgers and fries filled the air.

"I'm not sure that's true," she said casually, joining their conversation.

"I hope not," Jake replied. "Because we're trying to photograph one."

"My uncle saw one in Colville National Forest back in 2017. He swears on his life," she said.

Ajay leaned forward. "What did he see?"

"He was out hiking with four friends. It was the middle of the day. They'd gone off the trail and were spread out, exploring. He was in a clearing—trees all around with one big tree in the middle."

Both boys stared, transfixed with her story.

The waitress continued, "He heard some noises coming from the trees in the other direction—like twigs breaking, as if something was walking around. He looked over there, and just about 25 yards away, he saw this hairy thing, like 7 to 10 feet tall, standing in the bushes."

"What did it look like?" Jake asked.

"He said it had dark-brown, shaggy fur; thick shoulders; and piercing eyes."

"Wow . . . what'd he do?" Ajay asked.

"He hid behind the only tree in the clearing and watched it for about 30 seconds, kind of frozen. But then he bolted toward his friends. He heard the thing running through the trees, like he'd startled it. It was running away too."

"Was he sure it wasn't a bear?" Jake asked.

"He was totally sure," the waitress reassured. "He spends a lot of time outdoors and has seen all kinds of wild animals. But he'd never seen anything like that."

She scuttled off to tend to another patron.

"Eat up," Jake said, grinning at Ajay. "We've got a date with a Sasquatch in Colville National Forest."

Ape Canyon Bigfoot
Mount St. Helens, Washington
Summer 1924

Ranger William Welch and his colleague J.H. Huffman stood at the edge of the cliff, looking into the gorge.

"This is where we shot it," Fred Beck said, standing several feet back. "I could tell it was hit. Maybe three times? It staggered over to where you guys are standing and stumbled off the ledge."

William gave J.H. a side-eyed glance before turning to face Fred. "You fellas were out here hunting?" William asked.

"No, sir, just prospecting for gold," Fred replied. "We've been coming to this area for a while. You've got Spirit Lake about 8 miles over there." Fred pointed into the distant trees. "We built a cabin a ways off in that direction," he added, swinging his arm toward another area of dense forest.

"Must have had some luck finding gold up here if you built a cabin," J.H. said before returning his attention to the gorge below.

"Enough to keep us coming back, I suppose."

"And you say this thing you shot was 7 feet tall?" William asked.

"At least," Fred said. "There were four of them. They had to be around 400 pounds each. They stood upright, no different than you and me, except they were huge and covered in shaggy black fur from head to toe. And they had pointed ears that stuck up at least 4 inches from the tops of their heads."

William and J.H. exchanged glances.

"I'm telling you, that's what we saw," Fred insisted, sensing their doubt. He had to admit he would have doubted the story, too, if he hadn't witnessed it. But he had been there—right alongside his friends Gabe Lefever, John Peterson, Marion Smith, and his boy Roy.

"Why, exactly, did you determine you needed to shoot the thing?" William asked.

"I was afraid. They were so big. I've never seen anything like it, and I just . . . I don't know. I guess I just reacted. I panicked," Fred admitted with a sigh. "I regret it now."

"If this ape-man creature fell into the gorge, I say we go find its carcass," J.H. said. He'd worked as a ranger for a long time, and while he'd heard the legends of "mountain devils" from local Native Americans, he chalked it up to myth.

The three men spent more than an hour searching near the spot where Fred claimed the creature had fallen. They came up with nothing—not a drop of blood, a tuft of fur, or even broken branches in the undergrowth. They checked the ground for footprints with four toes, as the men had described, but again found nothing.

Fred led them through the thick forest to the small cabin. Little more than a shack, the structure bore some damage, which could have been signs of the attack that the men had claimed to endure the night before.

"Walk us through what happened," J.H. said, stepping through the threshold.

Several large rocks, varying in size, were spread across the cabin floor. A ray of sunlight beamed through a hole in the roof.

"We all went to bed," Fred began. "I'm not sure how long we'd been out before I heard a loud crashing sound that woke me up." Fred shivered at the memory.

He recalled thinking that someone or something was throwing its body against the wall and pounding at the door. The men all woke up; the assault on the cabin was so intense that whatever grip sleep might have had on them was quickly shaken off.

"We thought they might bust through the walls," Fred said. "I'm not sure how long this went on. It seemed like forever. They just kept pounding and throwing themselves into the walls. It sounded like they were throwing rocks at the cabin. Eventually, they got on the roof, tore that hole in it, and started throwing rocks at us." Fred motioned toward the hole, then nodded toward the rocks strewn around the room.

The rangers looked at the stones.

"One of them hit me in the head," Fred continued. "The guys said I was out cold for a couple hours."

"And you say, when the sun came up, the things took off?" William asked.

"Yeah. We waited awhile, then looked outside to make sure the coast was clear before we hustled back to town to report what happened."

The rangers walked around outside for a while, surveying the ground around the cabin. They found large footprints and measured them to be 14 inches long.

"I don't know," J.H. said. "They could have staged the rocks and made these footprints with their hands themselves."

He demonstrated by pressing the palm of his right hand and knuckles into the soft dirt. It wasn't a perfect match, nor was it as large, but it was close enough for J.H.'s satisfaction. The idea of ape-like humanoids attacking Fred and his mining buddies was more than J.H. could accept. He'd spent the afternoon investigating the area, trying to poke holes in the man's stories. He simply didn't want to believe it.

He knew he'd have to face reporters when he got back to the office. *The Oregonian* was sure to have gotten word by now. News traveled fast—especially news like this.

Fred could never have known that, 100 years later, his account would become deeply ingrained in the lore of Bigfoot, or that Washington would become the state with the most Bigfoot sightings. The gorge into which the beast reportedly fell would be named Ape Canyon, years later, because of the incident.

Despite J.H. and William publicly discrediting the account, Fred and the others who lived through it never wavered. They'd experienced something horrific on that fateful summer night in 1924. Whatever it was would haunt their memories for as long as they lived.

Idaho Bigfoot

Potlatch, Idaho
March 22, 2017

It was, by all accounts, a normal Wednesday evening. Fifty-year-old Stephanie finished a few tasks around the house before driving into town to pick up her husband, James, from work. After sliding into the driver's seat of their Subaru Forester, she turned the key in the ignition and glanced at the clock on the dashboard.

I should get there about 5 minutes early, she thought, pleased to be ahead of schedule.

She turned onto US-95 and started the familiar journey. The tires thrummed along the blacktop. The sun dipped behind the rows of pines that stood across the pasture, beyond the old farmhouse and barn.

Stephanie's headlights flipped on as dusk settled across the gentle rolls of land—not quite flat but not quite hills—which billowed like wrinkles in a blanket on an unmade bed. She adjusted the vehicle's temperature, _ver taking her eyes off the road. There was a chill in the air, as winter tried to keep its hold.

Something running along the side of the road caught Stephanie's eye. A deer raced through the ditch parallel to her. The white of its tail flicked in stark contrast to the browns and muted greens of the dusky countryside. There was an effortless grace in its strides, its head held high on a slender neck like a ballerina poised on a great stage.

Relieved that the deer wasn't in front of her, Stephanie returned her attention to the road for a moment before glancing at the deer again. An unsettling look of horror glinted in its eyes, and Stephanie felt a shiver run down her spine. She'd never seen such a look of fear in another living creature. It unnerved her.

That deer is running so fast, she thought. *What is it running from?*

That question was quickly answered when she looked into the rearview mirror. Bounding behind the deer was a creature covered in thick, dark fur—a deep brown bordering on black. It sprinted past bushes and trees along the roadside, and Stephanie could easily see that it was quite tall—maybe up to 8 feet. It bolted forward with long strides, less graceful than the deer but equally fast. Maybe faster.

Stephanie gasped, flipping her attention quickly to the road to ensure she stayed on it before looking into her mirror again, toward the scene playing out a few yards behind her. In that second, she realized the deer was out of view. She glanced ahead just as it crossed the road in front of her.

Stephanie hit the deer with a sickening thud.

For a moment, she thought the shriek she heard might be the deer—or worse, the thing chasing it. But she quickly realized that the scream was her own.

Oh, no, she thought, horrified. *That creature was right behind the deer.*

Her instinct to stop and assess the damage to the deer and her vehicle was overpowered by the fear that whatever chased the deer into the road might be within reach. She pressed the gas pedal and accelerated to speeds well beyond the posted limit.

Several minutes later, she pulled to a stop at the front door of her husband's office. Her knuckles were pale, and her fingers ached from gripping the steering wheel.

James came through the door but hesitated as he got closer to the vehicle. He detoured from his path to the passenger door and angled toward the hood.

Stephanie watched him step through the headlight beams. His shadow stretched across the parking lot. Tilting his head to one side, he reached forward and pulled a strand of tawny fur from a crack in the bumper. He opened the driver's-side door and looked at his wife.

"You okay?" he asked.

She nodded stiffly. "I hit a deer that was being chased by Bigfoot." Her voice was tight, and the words that came out sounded crazy, even to her.

James could tell by her expression that she was serious. "Let's drive over to the sheriff's office and make a report," he said. "You want me to drive?"

Stephanie scooted into the passenger seat, not wanting to step out of the vehicle, even though the creature was miles away. Her neck throbbed—most likely a mild case of whiplash from the collision.

The couple reported the accident to the Benewah County Sheriff's Office. Stephanie knew her story sounded unbelievable, but she also knew what she'd seen.

Local law enforcement took her report seriously. Stephanie thought they might have even believed her. In fact, the department went out to the scene and looked for signs of Bigfoot. This was Idaho, after all, and reports of Bigfoot were common enough to land the state on the top-five list of Bigfoot hot spots in the US. But the officers didn't find any conclusive evidence.

Stephanie's story never wavered, even when contacted by a journalist from the local paper. She agreed to share her story under the condition that she could remain anonymous. She wasn't looking for attention, but she felt it was right to warn others.

So watch out for any deer that cross US-95. You never know when one might be trying to outrun a sasquatch.

Batsquatch

Buckley, Washington
April 19, 1994

The door slammed shut behind 18-year-old Brian as he rushed into the house and hurried toward his parents' bedroom. At 10 p.m., Brian knew they'd already be in bed.

"Dad, go grab your gun and a camera. Come with me!"

"What's going on?" His mom's voice was thick with sleep.

"Brian, what on Earth . . ." his dad began.

"I gotta talk to you," Brian replied. His words caught in his throat as he tried to catch his breath.

His parents realized that something was seriously wrong and quickly followed their teenage son into the living room.

"What is it?" his mother asked, her words tight with worry.

Brian's face had gone pale, and his hair seemed to stand on end. His body was shaking, and he swallowed hard. He tried to find the right words. "I was driving home from Buckley, and my truck just stopped in the middle of the road. It didn't break down or anything—it just stopped. I couldn't figure out why." He took a slow, shaky breath. "And then this thing dropped out of the sky onto the road, right in front of my headlights."

"What kind of thing?" His father asked, his grogginess replaced by an alert sense of worry.

"First, I saw its feet coming down out of the sky. They were like giant bird feet with clawed toes. Then I saw a body covered in bluish fur. It had these broad shoulders with wings kind of folded behind its back. It was at least 9 feet tall."

Brian's parents listened, their eyes wide.

"Its face—oh, man, it was freaky. It had yellow eyes shaped like a piece of pie with pupils like a half-moon. It didn't have fangs, but its mouth was big with sharp, white teeth. Its face was like a wolf, but its ears were like tufts on top of its head."

"Are you sure?" His dad asked.

"I'm sure. It was only about 30 feet from the front of my truck, standing there in my headlights, looking at me, almost like it didn't know what to think of me."

Brian's mom reached out and took her son's hand. "We believe you," she assured him. She knew her son was an honest kid. If he said he saw a winged creature drop out of the sky, she was sure he had.

"I didn't feel threatened," Brian continued. "I just felt out of place. But it was staring right at me, like right through me. It just stood perfectly still." He shuddered.

Brian's dad got dressed, and the two hurried to a neighbor's house. This neighbor was deeply familiar with the woods, so if anyone could help them, it was him.

The trio drove to the site of Brian's encounter, armed with guns. They surveyed the road, looking for evidence of the creature, but they found nothing.

"You say it was standing right about here?" the neighbor asked, positioning himself in the center of the road.

"It stood there for several minutes. Then it just kind of twitched its fingers and unfolded its wings."

"How big were his wings?" his dad asked.

"As wide as the road," Brian replied.

"Dang," the neighbor said, almost to himself. "Then what did it do?"

"It turned its head, looked back at me, and started flapping its wings. Then it rose in the air, slowly. The wind from its wings made my truck shake. It flew toward Mount Rainier."

The three men looked toward the great mountain, squinting into the darkness, half hoping they might see the creature while silently praying they wouldn't.

"You said your truck stalled before you saw it. How'd you get home?" the neighbor asked.

"A few minutes after it flew off, my truck started again. I took off as fast as I could."

* * *

Over the next few days, word spread about what Brian had seen. While some of his classmates believed him, others started to make fun of him. One of his more artistically inclined friends helped him create a sketch of the creature. Soon, everyone was talking about "Batsquatch."

A local reporter interviewed Brian, his family, and their neighbors.

"It did happen. I'm willing to put my life on it," Brian told the reporter. "The truth is, I'm not really into this stuff. It boggles my mind really hardcore. It's weird. I don't like it."

The reporter found his story to be credible, albeit bizarre. It was clear that Brian was not trying to get attention and that the encounter had left him traumatized. Brian wished it never happened because he couldn't get the image of the creature out of his mind.

He wasn't the first to see the creature, and he wouldn't be the last. Others had reported the same sort of beast on Blue Horse Trail near Mount Saint Helens. Those accounts began after the volcano erupted on the morning of May 18, 1980.

While everything on the mountain was destroyed, something began to linger on the edge of the dead zone—something that brought with its presence an eerie silence. This unnatural kind of quiet seemed to pause the sounds of nocturnal bugs and critters.

While the eruption smothered the landscape with ash, bringing death to vegetation, animals, and 57 people, it seemed to awaken a beast that still wanders the nearby woods and flies through the night sky, haunting the area with its presence.

The Gumberoo
Kingston, Washington
1892

Jack scooted his chair closer to the potbelly stove. The 18-year-old stretched his arms back and propped up his feet, expertly balancing his body weight on the back two legs of the chair. It was the sort of thing for which his mother would have scolded him, but none of his logger bunkmates paid him any mind.

Every muscle in his body ached. The work was more difficult and dangerous than he could have imagined. But sending that first paycheck home to his family in Seattle made it all worthwhile.

He sniffed the air, then pulled his shirt over his nose in a halfhearted attempt to block out the fresh stench. While his muscles were finally getting used to the physical labor, he wasn't sure his nose would ever grow accustomed to the overwhelming odor of wet shoes and sweaty clothes that his bunkmates spread out everywhere in mostly futile efforts to dry them by morning.

Walter, his new friend who'd started on the same day, came over to their bunk and pulled up another chair. He seemed lost in thought.

"Have you heard of the gumberoo?" he asked Jack.

"No, what's that?"

George, lying atop the bunk next to theirs, chimed in. "The gumberoo is as fierce a creature as you could ever find in these woods."

George had been working as a bucker for the Big Creek Logging Company for more than a year. He'd proven to be a wealth of information for the new rookies.

"What does it look like?" asked Jack.

"Like a black bear without hair," said George. "Its hide is smooth and black and as tough as leather—and gumberoos are mean as hell."

"They live in the woods?" asked Jack, realizing, not for the first time, that as a city kid, he had a lot to learn about surviving in these woods.

"They burrow into the base of burned-out cedars. They spend most of their lives sleeping, but when they come out to eat, they are ravenously hungry."

"Have you ever seen one?" asked Walter.

"Nah," said George, "but I had a bunkmate who had a friend who tried to shoot one. The thing was so hungry it ate an entire horse and then went along looking for more. When the man shot it, the bullet bounced off the creature and back at him, hitting him square in the heart and killing him on the spot."

Jack rolled his eyes. "That's impossible."

George looked squarely at Jack. "You ain't calling me a liar, are you?"

"No, sir, of course not," said Jack in a rush. "I'm just surprised is all."

"Good," George said, breaking into a grin. "Why are you asking about the gumberoo, anyway?" he asked Walter.

"I think I smelled one today," Walter replied. "It was like burnt rubber. You can't mistake the smell of burnt rubber."

"Did you hear a pop and a bang just before?" asked George.

Walter thought for a moment. "I'm not sure . . . maybe? I suppose I could have."

"Well, lad, no matter. If you smelled it, then you've got nothing to worry about."

"Why is that?" asked Jack.

"Because the only thing that can kill a gumberoo is fire. When a gumberoo catches on fire, they explode. And when they explode, they leave behind a stench of burnt rubber." George turned over in his bunk, indicating that the conversation and lumber-camp lesson of the day was over.

Jack looked at Walter, who still appeared worried, and shook his head. He would never say it out loud, but he was sure that George was spinning a yarn. If there was a creature that looked like a hairless bear, was hungry enough to eat an entire horse, and exploded if it caught on fire, he surely would have heard about it before now—even in the city.

Flix, the Conser Lake Monster
Millersburg, Oregon
1959

The man driving the truck, filled with a haul of mint, was happy the day was almost over. It had been a long one. He drove through Millersburg, careful to maintain the speed limit.

As he cruised past Conser Lake, he thought about the local chatter. The town had been abuzz about a flying saucer that had reportedly crashed into the lake. When he glanced into his rearview mirror, he got the shock of his life.

Running behind his truck was a large, white, ape-like creature, standing 9 feet tall—and it was gaining on him. Soon, it caught up and peered through his window. The man glanced at his speedometer. He was going 35 miles per hour, yet the strange humanoid kept pace beside him. Horrified, the driver opted to kick up the speed, leaving the beast in his dust.

While this may have been the first reported sighting of a strange creature lingering near Conser Lake, it wouldn't be the last.

* * *

July 1960

The teens were intrigued by the reports of flying saucers and rumors of the truck driver's strange encounter. Such a creepy story already had the kids on edge, so the group's two pranksters decided to use their friends' fear—and the darkness of night—to their advantage.

They snuck away and hid, prepared to scare the pants off their pals. But as they waited in the darkness, a strange noise caused their hearts to race.

"What was that?" Franky asked.

"It was too loud to be human," said Sam.

To their horror, a 9-foot-tall creature moved out of the shadows and began rushing toward them. Its webbed feet seemed to squish against the pathway.

The boys' screams echoed into the night, as they ran away from the monster and back toward their friends. But the beast was on their trail. The pair dove into the bushes and held their breaths, praying the monster wouldn't find them.

As the stoop-shouldered beast hurried past, the duo heard it let out a strange sound.

Fleep . . . fleep-weep . . . fleep.

Sam turned on his flashlight.

"What are you doing?" Franky asked, terrified.

"Look at it. It's like a weird white bear running on two legs," said Sam.

"More like a giant white gorilla," Franky noted.

Whatever it was, the boys agreed: They needed to get home and call the police.

* * *

Sheriff George Miller wasn't sure what the boys had seen, but it had spooked them, and he was determined to get to the bottom of it. He took a small crew out to investigate.

"What exactly are we looking for?" a deputy asked.

"Something big, tall, and ghostly, I guess," the sheriff replied.

While officers scoured the area, they found no sign of the creature.

In the days that followed, more people descended upon the lake, hunting for the beast. Some carried shotguns and, in some cases, opened fire into the brush, making the whole ordeal even more dangerous. Some of the curiosity-seekers claimed to have seen the monster. A psychic allegedly communicated with it and announced that the creature's name was Flix. The name stuck, but the cryptid remained elusive.

Before long, the fear turned into a memory, and the story became a myth associated with the small community. Reports of the monster ceased, and the body of water, no longer known as Conser Lake, is as mysterious as the beast itself. While the lake was referenced in old newspaper articles, few seem certain which of the local ponds it was—and those who do know aren't telling.

Dogman
Twin Falls, Idaho
2017

Pastor Chuy stood in the church lobby, chatting with patrons as the sanctuary seats emptied. The service had been especially uplifting. Chuy was proud to be part of the team that shepherded the good people who called this place their church home.

"Another good service," Tobby said, smiling as he neared Chuy.

"Amen to that," Chuy replied, extending his right hand toward his parishioner. "Great to see you today. How's work going?"

"Not bad," Tobby replied. He was employed as a federal investigator within the department of environmental quality.

Chuy thought that was a cool gig—especially in a place like Twin Falls, Idaho. Nestled in the center of southern Idaho, Twin Falls offered some of the most beautiful wilderness spaces Chuy had ever seen. Snake

River Canyon brought nature enthusiasts from around the world. With a width of 10 miles and a depth of 7,913 feet, it was the deepest river gorge in the United States—and 2,000 feet deeper than the Grand Canyon.

Countless caves peppered the canyon walls, and Chuy sometimes wondered what might be hiding inside those dark, hollow spaces. Some were so remote and inaccessible that no human had likely ever seen inside.

The two men chatted as the church emptied and continued chatting as they made their way into the parking lot. Tobby's vehicle was parked near the front door. Chuy noticed the sticker on the back: a decal depicting the outline of a sasquatch, hunched shoulders with arms that seemed a bit too long, wisps of fur, and, of course, oversize feet.

"Are you a believer?" Chuy asked, nodding toward the sticker.

"I sure am," Tobby answered, unashamed. "I've done some research into Bigfoot and gathered a lot of information about eyewitness accounts, especially around the gorge."

"No kidding?" Chuy replied. "I've always been intrigued by Bigfoot." He paused for a moment, not wanting to sound crazy. He'd noticed some strange things in the small canyon not far from his home. But he was talking to a man who proudly displayed a Bigfoot sticker on his vehicle, so he continued. "Our house is just a few hundred yards from one of the canyons that splinters off the Snake River Canyon. The livestock commission is on the other side of us."

"Oh, yeah," Tobby replied, nodding. "I know where that is."

"Every now and then, one of the beef cattle will wander into the canyon. Of course, they're usually found right away and quickly led back to the pasture. But one night, I heard one of those cows screaming. It was coming from the direction of the canyon, and it was awful. It screeched in pain and made a terrible gurgling sound—like it was being eaten alive. I don't know what was happening, but it was one of the worst things I've ever heard."

Tobby listened intently. "You're not the only one who's heard that sort of thing. Other people have told me similar stories."

"What do you suppose it is?"

The men both glanced toward the decal.

"You'd be surprised what might be out there," Tobby replied.

"I'd love to hear about some of the stuff you've found in your investigations," Chuy said.

Tobby laughed. "I could yack at you for hours about all the stuff I've heard. Tell you what: I'll do you one better. Why don't we go out and do a little investigating together?"

"I'd love that," Chuy replied.

* * *

Not long after their conversation, the men met at Chuy's house before heading to the canyon for the afternoon.

"What a great location," Tobby said, gazing toward the ridge.

The land above the canyon was desert—the sandy, flat terrain a stark contrast to the lush green of the trees and bushes that thrived along the steep ridges below.

"We're lucky," Chuy replied. "My family loves to go walking and biking along the trails. We're not far from some nice little streams we can fish in. It's got everything."

The men jumped into Chuy's SUV and headed toward the main entrance on the opposite side of the gorge. They entered the canyon and walked along the trail. It wasn't long before they came upon some fencing and a "no trespassing" sign that had recently been put up.

"I was out here with my family one day, and we were exploring this area," said Chuy. "About a week later, when we came back, this was here. We thought it was odd."

"Interesting," Tobby said, eyeing the landscape beyond the fence.

"Then I heard that cow. The sound seemed to come from right around there," Chuy said, pointing toward the now-off-limits area.

Tobby shrugged. "I say we check it out." He smiled, holding up his credentials. "Perks of the job."

Chuy grinned back as the pair made their way into the fenced area. They walked for a while, listening to the sounds of bugs and birds. Occasionally, they paused to pick blades of grass and used them to whistle bird calls into the wind, sometimes getting a response from a far-off branch. The forbidden space felt much less foreboding beyond the gate and sign. It was calm and peaceful.

Until it wasn't.

The shift was abrupt, like an alarm clock waking them from a pleasant dream. A low growl emanated from beyond the trail—maybe 30 feet away. Somewhere in the thick brush and dense trees, something sounded angry.

The men exchanged wide-eyed glances before peering into the thicket.

"Could be a mountain lion," Chuy said, recalling a recent incident when one wandered into town.

"They aren't uncommon around here," Tobby replied. "That sounded pretty close."

Chuy nodded in agreement, his eyes still scanning the shadows of the woodland around them. He shifted his gaze upward and saw a tree, just a few yards away, with its bark shredded about 10 feet above the ground. It looked as if an angry grizzly bear had clawed at the trunk, tearing through the protective bark to expose the soft, white flesh of the tree—only there weren't grizzlies in this part of Idaho.

Tobby followed his gaze. "I think we'd better start making our way back to the entrance," he suggested.

Afternoon had turned into early evening, and they had traveled farther than they'd planned. The journey out seemed to take longer than the walk in, perhaps because they were more keenly aware that danger lurked.

Upon reflection, the men decided that the growl felt more like a warning than an immediate threat. After a while, they found themselves chatting once again about life and faith—maybe in part to distract themselves from the impending nightfall that was certain to swallow them before they could make it back to Chuy's vehicle.

"We should have brought flashlights," Chuy said as the last bit of sunlight dipped beyond the horizon.

"Yeah, the day got away from us," Tobby replied, pulling his phone from his pocket. "Shoot, only 10% battery life." He slipped it back into his pocket, looking around the trail as his eyes adjusted to the darkness.

"Mine's low too," Chuy said. "But I can see pretty well, now that my eyes have gotten used to it."

"I can too," Tobby agreed. "Let's save the phones in case we really need them."

Much of the trail was sparsely populated by trees, allowing for a considerable amount of moonlight to shine through. Other areas were shrouded in darkness by a canopy of trees hanging over the path. As the men walked through such an area, all the usual sounds of life that had been the background music of their hike abruptly stopped. The silence was eerie. It sent a shiver up Chuy's spine.

"It's really weird down here," Tobby said.

Chuy nodded and reached into his pocket, remembering he'd brought a pocketknife. The cool metal in his palm gave him a little solace but not much. He looked around for animal tracks: a few coyote prints, some racoons, no cougar—thank goodness.

That's when he noticed a large black mass, maybe 9 feet tall, that stood along the side of the trail about 60 feet in front of them. He wasn't sure what it was. He could only tell that it was dark and stood on two legs.

"Something just crossed the trail," Tobby said, his voice breaking the silence.

"I saw it," Chuy confirmed. His hand, still in his pocket, gripped the knife. He pulled it out and opened the blade as he turned on his heels, prepared to run.

"Don't," Tobby said sternly, grabbing Chuy's arm. "Showing fear will make it worse."

Chuy froze. His hand clenched the small knife, and he looked at Tobby, whose firearm was out of its holster and in his hand. Tobby peered into the forest where the creature had gone.

Another low growl, like the one earlier, emanated from the underbrush. The men began to back up slowly, each holding his breath as they listened.

Both knew that they had to continue forward. It was the only way to the vehicle, which wasn't far now. Weapons in hand, they pressed onward, through the tar-like darkness with who-knows-what lurking in the trees.

As they walked, they could hear something else walking, just off the path, parallel to them. The blood in Chuy's veins felt like ice. The men could barely see one another as they hiked side-by-side. When they paused, the nearby sounds of snapping twigs stopped. When they began again, the sounds resumed.

Chuy was terrified.

The canopy of trees above them seemed to stretch on forever, although only a few minutes passed before they stepped into the moonlit path beyond the tree line. The sound of snapping twigs and rustling underbrush was replaced with the soft chirping of crickets.

The men hurried to the car and drove to Chuy's home.

"Did that just happen?" Chuy asked, handing Tobby a glass of bourbon, already sure of the answer.

"Yeah, man, we saw it," Tobby replied. "It was at least 2 feet taller than me and had to weigh 400 pounds."

Chuy agreed.

The men were shaken, but safely at the house, the encounter seemed less frightening. They'd experienced something they couldn't fully explain. A calm settled over them as the bourbon warmed the chill of fear that had enveloped them.

Chuy had no way of knowing that this was the proverbial calm before the storm.

* * *

Roughly a week after Chuy and Tobby's strange encounter, the visitations began.

Chuy's wife was the first to notice. "Something was on our roof last night," she told him one morning. "There was a loud thump above us and then footsteps." Her brow furrowed. Confusion and disbelief etched her face. "At first, I wasn't sure I was fully awake. But I listened to it for a while, just kind of frozen."

An image of the dark creature from the canyon flashed into his mind. What if it had followed him home?

No, he thought, *that's crazy.*

He hadn't told his wife about the creature. He wasn't sure if that was because he didn't want to scare her or because he feared she'd think he was delusional. He hardly believed it himself. Yet he knew his experience was real.

He looked out the window. A layer of fresh snow blanketed the yard.

"I'll go on the roof and see if there are any signs of something up there."

To his surprise, he discovered strange, triangle-like tracks, barely visible under the snow that had mostly filled them in. They were obscured enough by the fresh flakes that he convinced himself they belonged to an owl.

He shared the theory with his wife.

"It sounded a lot bigger than an owl," she noted, but she accepted his conclusion. After all, what else could it have been?

Another week passed before it happened again. This time, at around 3 a.m., Chuy was the one awoken by noises on his roof. He got up and ventured down the hallway. Quietly, he peeked into his daughters' bedrooms. They were sleeping.

He moved through the house, checking all the windows and doors to make sure they were locked, as he listened for more sounds. All was silent.

The sun rose a few hours later, and Chuy went outside to have a look at the roof. More snowfall from the past week had filled in the tracks from before, so the white blanket across the rooftop should have been smooth. It wasn't. Fresh tracks stretched from one side to the other.

They were deep and clear—and unlike anything he'd ever seen in nature. The front of the prints was wide but narrowed to a point at the other end. They looked like dog tracks but . . . not. Something about them was almost human.

Chuy pulled out his phone and took pictures. Then he called Tobby and asked him to come over.

After showing him the prints, Chuy said, "I think Bigfoot followed me home."

"Those aren't Bigfoot tracks," Tobby replied, his expression heavy with worry. "Chuy, those are Dogman tracks."

Chuy had never heard of such a creature. He spent several hours over the next few days researching it and was shocked to find an account online very similar to his own. The witness reported the creature stalking across his roof, leaving behind a trail of triangle-like paw prints. Chuy's heart sank.

The odd events continued for weeks. His 8-year-old daughter was awoken around 3 a.m. by the sound of something tapping at her window. She described the noise as someone tapping with a rock. Chuy immediate thought that it wasn't a rock but a claw. He kept the horrifying thought to himself.

His research uncovered stories of these Dogman creatures trying to lure children out of their homes. That thought infuriated him.

Days later, his wife was working at her laptop on their patio when she was startled by something peering at her over their 7-foot-tall privacy fence. She rushed to Chuy, crying—confused and terrified by what she'd seen.

"It had to be 8 feet tall because its head was above the fence. It had a huge, black head—almost like a German shepherd with the pointed ears of a Dobermann. Its mouth was big and filled with white teeth." Her voice quivered as tears rolled down her cheeks.

Chuy rushed outside, but the creature was gone.

In that moment, he made a decision. He'd kept his experience in the canyon to himself, not wanting to scare his wife. But this beast was terrifying his family, and his wife needed to know why.

He told her everything. He felt gutted by guilt for letting this Dogman follow him home. Worse, he felt like a failure because he couldn't stop it from terrorizing his family. At least now there was relief in knowing they would fight it—whatever it was—together.

They installed floodlights and security cameras. They stayed cautious about when they let the kids go outside. Their guards were up.

Things remained calm after that, and Chuy let himself hope that the ordeal was over. One afternoon, he busied himself in his workspace in the garage, while the girls played in the yard. The calm broke.

"Dad!"

His daughters rushed into the garage, visibly upset.

"There was someone pounding on the fence," his oldest gasped.

"The whole fence was shaking!" the other exclaimed. "We thought it was you, playing a trick on us—but you're not out there."

Their eyes were round with fear, their voices tight.

Chuy hurried to the backyard, the girls trailing him. He looked everywhere, but no one was around. He tried to recreate what the girls experienced by shaking the fence, but no matter how hard he tried, the fence barely moved.

"It was probably just someone playing a prank," he told the girls, trying to calm their fears. But deep down, he knew it wasn't.

After that, Chuy and his wife were tempted to keep the girls inside at all times, but they knew they couldn't.

More time passed without incident.

One afternoon, Chuy took his older daughter for a bike ride on the canyon trail. They hadn't been there in a long time. She'd practically begged to go. She rode in front of him, her hair blowing in the breeze, a smile wide across her face.

She rounded a corner, just a few yards ahead of him.

Suddenly, he heard her scream. Her bike crashed onto the dirt path, and she kicked up rocks and dust as she rushed around the small bend, toward her father.

"What happened?" he asked, jumping from his bike and wrapping her in his arms.

She was shaking. "It tried to grab me!" She cried.

"What tried to grab you?" he asked, anger rising like fire in his gut. He already knew, but he needed to hear her say it.

"It was big and covered in black fur. It had a big snout and a huge neck."

Chuy reported the incident to Fish and Game. They went out with dart guns and rifles, looking for a black bear—but Chuy knew this was no bear. He also knew they weren't going to find it. The creature was too smart to be caught.

Whatever this was, it was evil. It wanted to terrorize him, and it seemed particularly focused on his children. The pastor had been through enough dark times in life to know that light always pushed away the dark, that God was more powerful than any Dogman.

His family cut branches from a plum tree in their yard. They formed crosses with the twigs and wrapped them in yarn to hold them in place. After anointing them with holy oil, they buried them in the four corners of their yard, praying that God would put a hedge of protection around their home.

Chuy had blessed homes for other congregants of the church. He believed in the power of the cross and the oil with which he anointed them. Above all, he believed in the power of faith, and his family trusted that God would protect them.

In the months that followed, the family heard screeches and howls coming from the canyon. Typically, he chalked them up to coyotes or wolves. But now and then, they sounded more like angry screams—like the Dogman was letting them know it was still out there, roaming deep in the wilds of the gorge.

His family never experienced a visit from the creature again. They were protected by faith, and that was a barrier even the Dogman couldn't penetrate.

Wendigo

Ashton and Pine Basin, Idaho Summer 2013

"Why do they call this place Warm River?" Andrew asked, stepping out of the camper and letting the thin door swing shut behind him.

"Because it never freezes," his grandfather replied. He set another log on the campfire and stoked it with a long, thick stick.

Andrew gazed at the river that flowed lazily beside the campground. He'd lived in Idaho his whole life, so he knew how cold the winters got. He imagined the river making its leisurely journey between snow-caked banks and pines dusted in white.

"That's pretty cool," Andrew replied.

His grandmother was busy putting away the remnants of dinner. They had spent the afternoon fishing along the banks, catching a few big enough to eat.

Camping with his grandparents had become a summer tradition; he and his brother looked forward to it each year. Fresh air and permission to roam the trails on their own—for two boys not yet in their teens, it was as close to independence as they got.

"Let's go," Jacob said, throwing the trailer door open with enough force to hit the camper wall.

"Easy, Hercules," their grandfather said with a wink.

"Enjoy your walk, boys, but be careful," their grandmother called after them.

Finding a place to watch the sunset had become part of the boys' nightly camping routine. On this evening, they hiked past thickets of willows and tall grass. Eventually, they came to a tunnel in the side of the mountain.

"I wonder what it's for," Andrew said as they walked through it.

"Maybe it's an old train tunnel," Jacob offered.

The smell of damp dirt filled the air as their feet crunched against pebbles. Their voices hit the walls, creating an echo as they spoke. They were more than halfway through the passage when they heard a screech that nearly made them jump out of their shoes. The tone had a metal-grinding-against-metal quality, yet it somehow sounded animalistic—a throaty, territorial warning cry from some creature neither boy had ever heard before.

Grabbing Andrew's arm, Jacob hurried toward the end of the tunnel, using words the boys would never say in front of their grandparents, but which seemed perfectly appropriate for the current situation.

Once on the other side, they paused to catch their breath and listened to make sure nothing was following them. The only sounds they heard were buzzing bugs and an occasional bird calling out from a nearby tree branch.

"What was that?" Andrew whispered.

Jacob squinted into the shadows of the passageway behind them. "I don't know, but I don't see anything in there," he said. "Let's keep hiking."

"We'll have to go through the tunnel to get back to the camper," Andrew said. His voice felt stuck in the back of his throat, as if fear had wrapped its hands around his neck and squeezed.

"By then, whatever that was will be long gone," Jacob said. His voice was calm and reassuring.

It wasn't long before the boys headed back. They hurried through the tunnel, keenly aware of every sound that echoed off its walls. They never heard anything menacing in there with them.

Before long, they were safely tucked away in the trailer for the evening, but Andrew struggled to sleep. He couldn't get the sound of that screech out of his head. Worse yet, he thought he heard whispers outside the camper.

"Do you hear that?" he asked, poking Jacob.

"Hear what?" Jacob groaned.

"Those voices."

It was the third time Andrew had jabbed his brother awake.

"I hear other campers talking. We're not the only ones camping around here. People are probably staying up late," Jacob replied with a sigh. "Now go to sleep."

The next day, the boys returned to civilization. The brief, odd encounter became a distant memory. Andrew convinced himself that his imagination overexaggerated it.

By the time the boys attended a family reunion at the Pine Basin ski lodge a few weeks later, the memory wasn't even a thought. The sun had set, and the boys were enjoying a game of Ghost in the Graveyard with their cousins. There were great places to hide outside the cabin, among the trees and undergrowth, close to the base of a nearby mountain.

"Here's a flashlight, so you don't get scared," Andrew's older cousin Scott said.

"I don't need it," Andrew protested as his cousins eyed the surroundings for a place to hide.

Being the youngest cousin wasn't always easy. Andrew wanted to be viewed as an equal, not the baby who needed a flashlight for night games. He tucked the light in his pocket and closed his eyes.

"One. Two. Three . . ."

The other children scattered. Twigs snapped beneath their shoes as they moved into their hiding places. Andrew listened, hoping to get an idea of the directions in which they'd gone.

When he finished counting, he searched in all the usual spots near the lodge. No luck. He ventured farther out toward the trees. As he peeked behind bushes and around thick tree trunks, he heard the familiar sound of a whistle—the same kind of whistle the kids made to give one another a clue as to where they were hiding.

Andrew smiled as he rushed toward the sound. He could hear his adult relatives laughing back at the lodge, not far away.

With each step, his excitement slipped away and was replaced by an overwhelming feeling of dread. He couldn't understand why, but suddenly he was scared. He wanted to find whoever whistled, so he wouldn't be alone in the darkness.

He was just a few steps from a large tree when he realized the laughing adults had gone silent. There was no buzz of crickets. There wasn't even the sound of a breeze rustling through leaves. Everything was completely and unnaturally still.

"I found you, Scott," Andrew cried, hoping his cousin would step out of his hiding place. "Come back to the lodge with me."

No one answered.

Anxious to get out of there, Andrew turned and began to walk away.

"You almost had me," a voice called from the trees.

"I knew it!" Andrew hurried back to the tree, flipping on his flashlight.

He expected to see his cousin. Instead, a creature stared back at him. Its skeletal body was long and cadaverous, like it had been dead and rotting for a long time—only it wasn't dead, not in the traditional sense, anyway. It was standing upright, its lifeless eyes set in the hollows of a face with skin stretched unnaturally tight across its jaw line. It was almost as if the creature was a skeleton, draped in flesh that was two sizes too small—ripped in some spots, rotting in others.

Andrew dropped his flashlight as he turned and sprinted down the hill toward the cabin. He heard the creature following, the underbrush crushed in the chase. The awful stench of rotting flesh seemed to envelop him as he ran.

When Andrew got to the lodge, weeping and out of breath, he told his family what he'd seen. None of the other kids had noticed anything unusual in the forest. But their parents kept them inside for the rest of the evening.

Once again, Andrew spent the night listening to odd sounds coming from around the lodge—as if the creature was just beyond the walls, taunting him while it watched and waited.

At the time, Andrew had no concept of a creature known as the Wendigo. It wasn't until many years later, when he saw one depicted in a video game, that he realized what he'd encountered. Even now, Andrew can't help but wonder if the beast is still out there, silently stalking kids in the darkness.

The Basket Ogress

Seattle, Washington
1967

Vi Hilbert walked toward the front door of Nooksak elder Louise George's home, a sense of excitement bubbling through her veins. A member of the Upper Skagit tribe, she was proud of her heritage. When Thom Hess—a linguist compiling a collection of Lushootseed-language songs and stories—asked to meet with her, she was intrigued.

Vi learned the native language from her parents as a child. She recalled asking them to speak their native tongue around her because she loved how it sounded. She also loved to see their smiles when she spoke to them in Lushootseed. It delighted them that she wanted to learn it.

Thom had told Vi that he was working with Louise on a recording of Vi's mother sharing the native legend of the Basket Ogress. They had agreed to meet at Louise's home.

Louise opened the door and welcomed Vi.

"We're glad you could come, Taqwseblu*," said a man, peering over Louise's shoulder. "I'm Thom Hess."

"Thank you for inviting me," Vi replied. She was pleased to hear him speak her traditional Lushootseed name. He'd even pronounced it correctly, which was impressive.

The trio sat at a table. Thom pressed play on a recorder, and there was Vi's mother, speaking from some distant time and place. The beautiful language Vi had grown to cherish reverberated through the speakers.

Vi felt warmth and pride as she listened to her mother share a story that Vi knew well. All Skagit children did. It was one that served to keep them in line: the story of an ogress who had a taste for misbehaving children.

Some believed the woman was a sasquatch. Tall enough to tower over children and adults alike, she traveled with a large, woven basket on her back. This was where she stored the naughty children. Often referred to as the Wild Woman of the Woods and Shores, the Basket Ogress was known up and down the Northwest Coast and played a role in countless stories.

This one, like so many others, featured children disobeying their parents. Despite being told not to, the children traveled away from home, a voyage downriver in canoes. One of the children had a severely curved spine that caused him to slouch, and the other children treated him poorly.

When they camped along the shore each night, they cooked fish over a fire. However, the children did not share the meaty portions of the fish with the slouched boy. They only gave him the tails.

After several nights of this treatment, the boy told the others, "If you're unkind to me again, I'll call out to the ogress to deal with you."

When evening came, he was only given the tails again. He cried out for the ogress to come. She was happy to oblige.

The giant woman stomped through the forest with her woven basket strapped to her back. When she arrived at the camp, she grabbed each child and put them into the basket, starting with the boy who had summoned her.

The children knew well what the ogress had planned. They'd heard stories of her hunger for children. Horrified by the situation he'd created, the boy pushed his way to the top of the basket. He watched the forest trees pass above them, the moon casting light through their branches. Whenever they passed under a low-hanging branch, he reached for it. He missed time and again—until, finally, he grabbed one and managed to escape.

When the ogress arrived home, she placed rocks on the fire to heat them, so she could cook her dinner upon them. After emptying her basket, she realized the boy who had summoned her was gone. Furious, she ran back and looked for him. She found him in a canoe, paddling away from shore.

The ogress grabbed rocks and threw them at the boy, hoping to stop him and reclaim him as her meal. But she missed every throw. Frustrated, she returned to her home, salivating at the thought of the other children she would soon eat.

As the children crouched in a corner, watching the ogress stoke her fire, they whispered to one another, plotting how to escape.

The ogress asked, "What are you saying?"

The children replied, "We are glad you will have such a wonderful meal. We would love for you to sing and dance before you cook us."

The ogress had never received such a request. "I'd be happy to!"

The giant woman sang and twirled and stomped her feet. As she did, the children cheered. Flattered by their enthusiasm, she continued with her performance.

Meanwhile, the children made their plan. They would push her into the fire and let her roast. When she got close to the children, they rushed at her. She fell onto the hot rocks, screaming for the children to get her away from the fire.

She pointed them toward a forked stick to save her. Instead, they used the stick to hold her down until she perished.

The recording ended. Vi sat back in the chair, a smile curling the corners of her mouth.

"How can I help?" she asked.

"We want to preserve the stories of your people," Thom answered. "We have recordings that we need help translating."

Vi's smile grew. This was the beginning of her life's work. Translating, sharing, and teaching the stories of the Skagit people would become her legacy—and it all began with a monster that hunted the woods of the Pacific Northwest, eliciting fear in the hearts of Skagit children. The legend of an evil ogress bent on eating children drew out a passion in Vi that had been simmering quietly under the surface her entire life.

Sometimes even monsters can bring out the best in people.

The Wampus Cat
Clark Fork, Idaho
Spring 1933

Shirley climbed the tall metal gate that blocked off the cattle pasture, and she perched at the top. The 10-year-old hooked the heels of her favorite cowboy boots into a metal slate and used her hands to balance as she gazed across the field. Her parents allowed her to venture to the neighbor's ranch, and this freedom seemed like one of the greatest things a kid could get.

Eunice and Robert lived at that ranch alone, their children grown and moved away to raise their own little ones. The couple treasured Shirley's visits as much as she did.

"Hey there, Shirley," Robert called, walking toward her from the barn.

"Good morning," she replied with a smile.

Shirley stopped by every Saturday to visit. Sometimes, Robert would give her a chore and pay her a nickel. Other times, Eunice would send her home with a fresh-baked cobbler.

Every Saturday, Robert would ask her the same question. "Have you seen any Wampus Cats lately?"

"No, sir, but I sure did hear them last night. They were howling like mad," Shirley said.

"Must've been on the hunt," Robert replied.

Shirley didn't know anyone who'd ever seen one of the mythical creatures, but everyone knew the eerie sounds they made.

She gazed toward the expanse of trees just beyond Robert and Eunice's ranch. "I wonder if I'll ever see one."

"Likely not," Robert replied. "They tend to hide in caves and hollowed-out trees of the forest. They only come out to hunt long after you've gone to bed, young lady."

"Sometimes, I stay up and read in the moonlight," she admitted with a grin. "Don't tell my dad."

"I think we can keep that secret between us."

Shirley loved Robert and Eunice like her own grandparents. The feeling was mutual. Robert had told the girl about the early Native tribes that lived in Clark Fork Valley, long before Clark Fork became a town. They were brave and feared almost nothing—but the Wampus Cat was such a fierce predator, it made even the bravest men and women's blood run cold.

The Wampus Cat was said to look similar to a cougar but with the face of a bobcat. Its long tail was a weapon—a spike-covered ball at the end, which it used to attack its prey. It was fast and stealthy, with long claws and even longer fangs. In this area, the Wampus

Cat reigned supreme. The Native Americans deeply respected its sovereignty over the land.

The local high school adopted the legendary feline as its mascot. Images of the cat around the school replaced its spiky tail with a basketball. Shirley found that more funny than fierce.

"My dad was reading the newspaper this morning and saw an article about the Wampus Cat," she said. "It warned people vacationing from the East Coast to watch out because the Wampus Cats are on the prowl after such a long winter. The article said people saw some of them running in a pack by the Boise River." Shirley paused. The furrow in her eyebrow showed her confusion. "I thought they always hunted alone."

"Those cats must be extra hungry after all the snowstorms," Robert offered. "I saw that story too. I read it while I drank my morning coffee."

"The paper said one was seen chasing a mountain lion and another was climbing a tree, going after a porcupine." She wrinkled her nose. "They must be really hungry if they want to eat something so prickly."

"I suppose they are," Robert said, leaning against the gate and looking across the pasture. "I hope they don't get a taste for my cattle."

"If they do, the paper said you need a claw hammer to rip out their fangs. The supply store ordered a lot of them for the easterners who are coming out this way."

"I've got a few of those handy in the shed," Robert said confidently. "We were always told that the males were damn near indestructible. But if it's a female, the best defense against a Wampus was to tackle them with a cross saw."

"I hope you never have to," Shirley said. The thought frightened her.

"Don't you worry about those Wampus Cats. I've always found that the best way to avoid trouble with them is just to be respectful. If you hear one, keep yourself inside. I'll do the same. We can replace a heifer or two, but we can't replace you or me." He winked.

That made Shirley feel better. Her smile returned.

"You didn't come over just to talk about Wampus Cats, did you?"

"Of course not," Shirley beamed. "I came to work."

"Well, then, get off that gate and come with me to the barn. We've got some cleaning to do in the hayloft. And I happen to know Eunice whipped up a fresh cherry cobbler—your favorite."

Baxbakwalanuxsiwae

Port Angeles, Washington
Fall 2023

Tanya dug through her pack to make sure she had her critically important headlamp. Satisfied it was there, she zipped the pack closed and hefted it onto her back. Today's outing was going to be easy–just a day hike. She slammed the car hatch closed and clicked the key fob to lock it.

Sam, who had been filming the trailhead marker of Striped Peak Trail, turned the camera to Tanya. "This should be a fun one," he said.

"Yes," agreed Tanya. "I'm excited for the views."

Tanya had met Sam just after college. They both shared a passion for exploring abandoned buildings and locations. They had started collaborating on a series of videos, examining forgotten histories, that was taking off online. Now they were on a scouting mission for a documentary.

This particular episode was going to be about the history of Camp Hayden, featuring the series of abandoned World War II bunkers that made up the coastal defense system during the 1940s. Tanya and Sam were trying to find the best places at which to come back and film with their crew.

The duo had already hiked several trails that provided access to some abandoned bunkers. But according to this hike's descriptions, it promised especially great views of the Strait of Juan de Fuca.

Tanya and Sam set off, and it wasn't long before the trail took them up in elevation.

"I'm a little worried that Henry is going to struggle here," said Tanya, taking a minute to catch her breath.

Henry was their cameraman, who readily admitted that he was overweight and out of shape.

"Yeah," agreed Sam, stopping behind her. "But it will be good for him."

They continued, hiking farther up to the promised views.

Stepping out of the treeline, Tanya didn't hide her awe. "This is incredible."

"We're literally on the edge of the country," Sam said, pointing across the water. "That's Canada."

"The edge of the country is why there was a defense system," said Tanya. "I always understood why they had a military presence here after Pearl Harbor, but it makes even more sense when you see it for yourself." She slapped a mosquito that landed on her arm.

"You know," said Sam, "there's a legend about a monster that lives in these woods."

Tanya laughed. "Really?"

Sam continued, "We're in the farthest northwestern corner of the country, right?"

Tanya nodded. "That anyone could reach."

"Then we are in Baxbakwalanuxsiwae territory. He lives in a remote cabin in the woods around here. His cabin is covered in red cedar bark, and blood-red smoke is always seen coming from the chimney."

Tanya scanned the horizon. "I don't see any blood-red smoke, so that's a good sign. What does he look like?"

"Some stories say he looks like an ogre. Others say he's more like an ugly bear—or even that he has hundreds of mouths all over his body with horrible gnashing teeth."

Tanya tried to imagine what a creature with 100 mouths might look like.

Sam continued, "According to legend, he may have once been a man. He was a cannibal, so he was cursed by the Kwakwaka'wakw, the early Indigenous tribe that roamed the area. They called him the Cannibal-at-the-North-End-of-the-World. His mouths all yell, 'Hap, hap, hap,' which means, 'eat, eat, eat.'"

"Interesting," said Tanya.

Sam smiled. "It's not often I get to tell you something you don't already know. I'm going to enjoy this."

Tanya rolled her eyes.

Sam continued, "Supposedly, his wife appears as a human. She and their servant, who also appears as a human, lure passersby to his home. They make the guests feel welcome and cook a large meal to help them feel comfortable. But when their visitors fall asleep, he comes and eats them."

Tanya shook her head. "It's always the remote cabins in the woods that you have to look out for." She was always up for camping, but as a city girl from L.A., she preferred the modern conveniences of a hotel.

"Supposedly, one day, a shaman wandered into his area," said Sam. "The cannibal and his wife tried to trick the holy man and eat him. Instead, the shaman got away and lured them both into a pit, where he set them on fire."

Tanya's eyes grew wide as she thought about their nearby campsite. "I think I'm going to have nightmares tonight."

Sam laughed. "I should have saved this for the campfire, but do you want to hear the best part?"

Tanya looked at him. "There's more?"

"Oh, yeah," said Sam. "The ashes turned into mosquitos and flew off into the world to devour as many people as they could in an attempt to satisfy their need for human blood."

"And there it is," said Tanya, feeling a little relieved that the story was over. She punched Sam on the arm. "Of course, the legend must have been invented to explain why a horrid little creature like a mosquito would exist."

"I'll think of something better for the campfire," he joked. "Have you heard about the ghost of the lady who haunts the lake?"

"Please, no," begged Tanya. "You know I'm terrified of ghost stories."

Sam got a gleam in his eye. "It's a good one. I promise."

"Storytime is over," announced Tanya. "We've got to go find our bunker." She marched toward the trail, not waiting to see if Sam would follow.

That's when she noticed a woman on the trail, who smiled and offered her a friendly wave. Behind her, in the distance, clouds of blood-red smoke wafted into the air.

Monster Creatures of the Water

Lake Chelan Dragon
The Coast of Washington
1812

The sea captain looked at the small chest on the table next to his bed and gave it an affectionate pat. His precious cargo had traveled far. It wouldn't be much longer until they reached their destination.

He glanced out the tiny circular window that he had propped open, and he stretched his nose up to sniff. He could smell a storm coming, and he was nervous about it. His nose was never wrong, and he hadn't smelled a storm like this in a long time. It was going to be a big one.

His thoughts turned to his last visit home in Saint Augustus. He and his father had walked beside the big lake, just as they had done when he was a child. He cherished those childhood memories. He liked to think they inspired his life at sea. No matter where he sailed, he was chasing that old feeling of exploring along the shores of Loch Ness.

During their walk, he told his father about all he'd seen in the world. His father responded by telling him that he'd been chosen to deliver a very special treasure. He was given the chest and was entrusted with a secret he'd carry to his grave. He hadn't expected the honor.

His crew assumed the small chest contained gold and jewels. They were wrong. He gave the chest another pat. It was much more than that.

The boat lurched. Instinctively, the captain knew the storm would arrive faster than expected. He stared at the chest and contemplated leaving it, knowing deep within that he probably should. But he hadn't let the chest out of his sight so far; it wasn't hard to carry around. And while he trusted his crew, they were human. Curiosity and greed could easily overtake loyalty. Deciding not to risk it, he tucked the chest under his arm and left the safety of his cabin to see about the storm.

He stepped onto the deck and was caught off guard by a gust of wind. It was so strong that it threatened to knock him off his feet. He grabbed the railing to keep from falling. Slowly, he made his way toward the front of the ship, all the while clutching the precious box.

He saw his first mate manning a line at the nearest mast. "Fergus!" the captain called, but his shouts were swallowed by a gale of wind.

The boat gave another lurch, and the precious treasure slipped from under his arm. It bounced once and then tumbled off the deck, into the sea.

"It's not the right place," screamed a voice inside his head.

Without hesitation, the captain dove off the boat and into the water.

* * *

Fergus secured himself with a rope and used all of his strength to hold tightly to the line he was manning.

Seeing the captain, he steadied himself and tried to wave him away. To his utter surprise, the captain dove off the deck and into the sea. Before Fergus could comprehend what his eyes had seen, two young women shoved their way out from behind several barrels that hadn't fit in the cargo hold.

Dumbfounded, Fergus realized the women must have been aboard since the ship had left shore several days earlier. His brain tried to imagine how the stowaways—two women—managed to stay hidden for so long.

"The egg!" shouted one.

"We have to save it!" shouted the other.

Both women dove off the deck after the captain.

Fergus watched in disbelief as their legs morphed into tails and the women swam deep into the sea.

Moments later, one returned to the surface, holding the chest above her head. She was followed by the other, who carried the ship's sputtering captain. The mermaids deposited him safely on board but took the chest and swam off into the storm.

Fergus and the captain himself would spend the rest of their lives perplexed, never quite sure how to explain the rescue and wondering what happened to the mystical egg.

According to legend, the egg was safely delivered to Lake Chelan. At nearly 1,500 feet deep, it was the third-deepest lake in the country and was 55 miles long—the perfect home for the new hatchling. With underwater caverns and plenty of fish to eat, not to mention rumors about underwater connections to other lakes and even the Pacific Ocean, a water dragon might thrive there, unnoticed.

* * *

Lake Chelan, 1892

Charles and his friends were enjoying a fall camping trip at what was known as Devil's Slide at the northern point of Lake Chelan. Charles waded into the water to clean his muddy feet. The water was cold, but it was the only way to rid himself of the thick, sludgy muck.

Suddenly, something bit his ankle.

Panicked, he shouted, "Something's got me! I need help!"

As the thing tried to pull him deeper into the water, he lost his balance and fell.

Michael and Robert splashed into the water, and each grabbed an arm. They yanked, but the thing yanked back. Charles worried that he'd be torn in half.

The men kept tugging. Slowly, they made progress, dragging their friend toward the shore with the monster still clamped onto his leg. As they reached the edge of the water, they saw the monster more clearly. It was mostly white and had large, webbed wings with leather-like skin.

The thing would not let go.

The men dragged their friend and the attached beast all the way up to shore and over to their campfire. Careful to keep Charles away from the flames, they attempted to burn the monster off their friend. That just seemed to irritate it.

The creature stretched out its long wings and lifted into the air, Charles's leg still held in its teeth. The men watched helplessly as it—and Charles—flew upward and away from them. When it was safely over deep enough water, the creature dove straight down and into the lake with its prey.

Charles was never heard from again.

Colossal Claude

Clatsop County, Oregon
March 15, 1934

C aptain J. Jensen stood aboard the *Rose* as the ship made its way across the Columbia River, toward the lighthouse at the mouth. It was, by all accounts, a normal day. The sky was clear, and the shipmates were carrying on with their duties across the ship, ensuring a safe journey.

As Jensen looked across the great expanse of water, movement near the ship caught his eye. Rising above the surface was a large head, almost like that of a camel, atop a thick, 8-foot-long neck.

The first mate, L.A. Larson, called from the boat deck, "Captain, do you see that?"

"I do," Captain Jensen confirmed with a nod, his eyes transfixed, watching the spectacle swimming casually near them.

"It's got to be 40 feet long," Larson said with a mix of fear and awe.

Sailors began to gather on the deck. Their murmured exchanges also filled with admiration and fright. Some ran to get field glasses for a closer look. Part of the creature's body could be seen above the water: a large round mass of tan flesh, trailed by a long tail.

The creature seemed equally as fascinated by them. It swam around the boat for several minutes, considering them with its large eyes. There was no sense of aggression from the beast. It just bobbed about curiously in the water.

"Let's launch a boat out and get closer," one of the men suggested.

"That creature's big enough to capsize our small boats. We're safe here, so here is where we'll watch it from," Captain Jensen replied.

After about 20 minutes, the mysterious sea monster drifted away and out of view.

* * *

It wasn't until 1937 that another reported sighting of the creature—which became known as Claude—emerged. It came from a crew of fishermen in that same area. They described the beast similarly, except they believed its body was covered in hair.

Many sightings followed, with witnesses spotting Claude from shorelines and off ship decks. It seemed that this section of water, just off the Columbia River Bar, had its own resident sea monster.

By the mid-1950s, sightings had ceased. Claude had perhaps moved away or passed on, as all living creatures must eventually do. But Claude undoubtedly left his mark and lives on as a local legend.

Devil's Lake Monster

Lincoln City, Oregon
Summer 2022

The fire crackled quietly in the rusted metal ring. Janice and Sarah set out a spread of chocolate bars, graham crackers, and marshmallows on the weather-worn picnic table. Bryan and Ben dropped a stack of branches and twigs a few feet from the fire.

"You guys are such wonderful hunter–gatherers," Janice teased.

"Gatherers maybe. I'm not sure about hunters," Sarah added. She secured the twisty tie onto the bag of hotdog buns left over from dinner. Then she tossed the remaining franks into the cooler, snapped the lid shut, and dropped herself onto the tabletop beside the s'mores supplies.

"You ladies are turning into my mother," Ben teased back, nodding toward the neatly displayed dessert supplies.

"I'm taking that as a compliment," Janice replied, slipping two marshmallows on a metal roasting stick. "Your mom is actually pretty cool."

"And very organized," Sarah added.

The two couples, all in their early 20s, had been planning this camping trip at Devil's Lake State Recreation Area for weeks. This was the women's first time sleeping under the stars near Devil's Lake, but Ben and Bryan had grown up in the area and had camped in the park several times.

They'd chosen this lot because of its proximity to the lake. They couldn't see the water—a fact that had disappointed the ladies, but they could hear it gently lapping against the shoreline, as a breeze rustled through the leaves around them. The moon was nearly full in the cloudless sky. Stars winked through the canopy of green above them.

Devil's Lake was a popular destination for people to enjoy nature. Only a small canal of water separated the freshwater lake that spanned 685 acres from the Pacific Ocean. Anglers and water-sports enthusiasts alike flocked to the area

"It's so peaceful here," Sarah said, settling into a popup chair beside Bryan.

Janice and Ben sat next to one another on the bench of the picnic table.

"The name—Devil's Lake—is super creepy," Janice added. "Why would they call it that?"

"Because of the monster in the water," Bryan said, matter-of-factly.

Sarah rolled her eyes. "Sure," she said.

"No, seriously," Ben said. "Way before it was a state park, this area was prime hunting ground for a Nakota tribe. They had a run-in with a sea creature that killed several men."

"They called the lake M'de Wakan—which I think means bad spirit or mystery lake," Bryan added.

"According to the legend, the chief coordinated a hunting trip one evening, sending a canoe full of warriors across the lake to an area known to be a really good hunting ground," said Ben.

Sarah stared wide-eyed at him across the small campfire, intrigued.

"The men paddled several yards into the water when, suddenly, huge tentacles reached out of the lake and wrapped around their canoe."

Janice gazed through the lines of trees between them and the shoreline. She and the others had just been standing on the fishing dock a few minutes ago, watching bluegills pop above the surface to eat bugs. The lake shimmered like black glass under the moonlight. Janice could imagine the canoe gliding across, just as they had that afternoon on paddle boards. A shiver ran down her spine as she thought that something monstrous could have been lurking beneath them as they laughed and enjoyed the sunshine.

"The men were screaming as this thing twisted the canoe in a death grip. Members of the tribe watched from shore in horror as the canoe was flipped and then dragged underwater with all the men still in it."

Janice's marshmallow caught on fire. She pulled in toward her and puffed out the flame.

"For decades, the tribe returned to the lake every year, giving an offering to the creature. They hoped to appease it, so it would spare their lives."

"Maybe you could've told us this before we spent all day splashing around in there," Sarah said, a little freaked out.

"If we had, you wouldn't have gone past the shoreline," Bryan said before taking a bite of his gooey chocolatey marshmallow treat. "Besides, that was like 200 years ago, so I'm pretty sure whatever that was is long gone now."

"Yeah, *that* monster has been dead a long time, but . . ." Ben's voice trailed off. He popped a roasted marshmallow into his mouth.

"But what?" Janice asked, raising an eyebrow.

"Well, in 1950, they found a different monster washed up on the shore," Ben replied. "A girl named Marybelle came across a carcass of something she described as being 4 feet long and roughly the same width. She said its body and legs were covered in hair or feathers, she wasn't sure which. It had nine tentacle-like things—some people described them as tails. One was really long—like 18 feet. The rest were at least 3 feet long, and some were about a dozen feet long."

"That sounds almost like a weird, hairy octopus," Sarah said.

"It kind of does." Ben shrugged and continued. "Marybelle's father served as the town marshal. He investigated the creature and said it weighed around 1,000 pounds.

"By the time Marybelle found the thing, it was dead. But apparently some other guy had come across it the day before and said, when he kicked it, it wiggled around a bit, like it might have still been alive."

"Gross." Janice shuddered.

"A bunch of locals came out to get a look," Bryan added. "They tried to haul it away with a wrecking car, but the thing was so heavy, it broke the line. They tried again and finally got it away from the water. People were touching it and cutting into it with knives. They said it felt kind of squishy like a snake, and the meat under the tan flesh was white."

"Yummy, lake monsters—the other white meat," Bryan quipped.

Ben laughed.

"I think we can pack up the paddle boards because there is no way I'm going back on that lake," Janice said firmly.

"Nope, me neither," Sarah added. "I'm really glad our campsite isn't right next to the water—where creepy, hairy octopus monsters apparently live."

Swan Valley Monster

Swan Valley, Idaho
August 22, 1868

Jed and his brother, Isaac, were fixing the fence in the south pasture when they saw the man running up the road. Jed had seen him in town before but didn't know who he was or what he might want. Curious, they abandoned their task to see what was going on.

"You have to come," said the man. "Bring your wagon." He stopped to catch his breath. "We need at least six men to help lift it."

"What are you talking about, old-timer?" asked Isaac. "I can't spare six men right now just because you say so."

"Trust me," the elderly gentleman replied, looking Isaac square in the eyes. "You'll want to see this."

"What is it?" asked Jed. "What's so important?"

"It's a monster, the likes of which I've never seen."

"A monster, you say?" Jed asked, his tone revealing his doubt.

"Where?" asked Isaac.

"Olds Ferry." The man's breathing was almost back to normal. "I was crossing the river there, and I saw a sea serpent."

"What did it look like?" Jed asked.

"It had a trunk like an elephant that was pointed up, and it was shooting water from it. Then its head poked out of the water. It was at least the size of a washtub, and it looked like a giant snake head, except it had a horn on top and long dark whiskers on both sides of its face—and fangs! It had fangs too."

Jed tried to picture the creature but couldn't. It was all he could do to keep from laughing.

"Anything else?" asked Isaac.

Jed could tell from Isaac's tone that he didn't believe the man either.

"Yes," said the man. "It was at least 20 feet long."

"How could you see that if it was in the water?" Jed asked.

"It crawled onto shore. It was sort of a green color with red-and-black spots."

"Red and black, you say?" a farmhand chimed in with a grin.

"Yes, sir." The man didn't seem to realize that no one believed him. "And it had little wings, like fins, and a spine along its back—sharp, pointy things like a porcupine. And claws. And a red tongue that shot out poison."

"Poison?" Jed asked, unable to hide a grin of his own.

"What did you do?" asked Isaac.

"I shot it," said the man, "first in its eye, but that just made it mad. So I shot it again in the belly. Still, it came at me, but then it fell over, spitting poison everywhere. It died, but that thing stinks to high heaven. It's a smell worse than death. I will never forget that smell as long as I live."

A half-dozen men had come to see what was going on and found themselves listening to the strangest tale they had ever heard.

"You have to come," continued the man, "and we need a wagon. You have to help me move it. People will want to see this!"

The men turned to Isaac to see if he would give his approval.

He nodded. "You and you." He pointed at two men. "Get the wagon."

They hurried off to complete their task.

"The rest of you, let's go."

Together, the newly formed posse walked the man back to the river. When they got close, Jed was struck by the foulest stench he had ever smelled—a smell that promised something worse than death.

Next to him, his brother started to heave and vomit. "I can't go," he whispered. "I can't smell that for another minute."

Behind them, the horses dug their hooves into the ground and refused to move the wagon forward. The driver encouraged them along, but they wouldn't budge.

The rest of the group continued to venture toward the riverbank, following the man.

Jed was excited to see this bizarre creature, which couldn't possibly be real—except that the foreign stench had to come from something. That part of the man's story was true. Could the rest of his description be real too? Jed suddenly wasn't sure that he wanted to know.

The elderly gentleman stopped in his tracks. "It was here," he said, pointing at a strange spot on the ground where the vegetation had died.

A trail of slime led back to the river.

"I swear. It was right here. I ain't never seen nothing like it, but where could it have gone?"

The man's story was so fantastical that it couldn't be true, could it? But the other-worldly stench was so pungent that his brother vomited, and the horses refused to follow. And the slime trail was tangible evidence of some sort.

For the rest of his life, Jed thought about the serpent-like creature and the old-timer's tale every time he ventured anywhere near the Snake River. It was impossible not to wonder if the creature had somehow survived and was perhaps lurking at the bottom of the deep pool of water.

Cadborosaurus – "Caddy"
Oak Harbor, Washington
June 1935

Gino took one last drag off his cigarette and tossed it aside. He studied it on the ground and noted how completely foreign it looked, lying on the beach among the rocks and sand. He felt a pang of guilt that surprised him. He never expected to care or even think twice about nature. He was a city boy from Jersey.

He trudged over to where he'd thrown the anomaly, his boots crunching the sand and leaving deep footprints. He picked up the evidence of his tobacco habit and decided to find a better place to dispose of it later.

When he had arrived the year before, he hated everything about nature. But after the stock market crashed and the economy was hit by what everyone started calling the "Great Depression," he had been lucky to get a job with President Roosevelt's brainchild, the Civilian Conservation Corps (CCC)—even if it meant having to live in nature.

He and about 200 other young men were assigned to work on the Deception Pass bridge-and-park project. Most, like him, sent the paychecks home to their families.

He looked up to where the bridge stretched across the sky, connecting his side of the world—his camp at Cornet Bay—with the CCC camp at Bowman Bay. The bridge looked across the Salish Sea and Cadboro Bay to the San Juan Islands and Vancouver Island.

The workers on his side of the bridge were all from the East Coast, mostly New York and New Jersey. The other camp was filled with locals. He'd always thought of them as cowboys and lumberjacks. In the beginning, they had to remain separated or fights would break out. But after months of working through all kinds of weather on the various park projects, like outbuildings, roads, trails, and especially the bridge itself, they couldn't help but become comrades of a sort. A man didn't put his blood and sweat into creating the things they'd made without learning to tolerate—and maybe even care about—his coworkers.

He lit another cigarette and looked across the water. He hated to admit it, but he was going to miss this place.

A flash of movement caught his eye. Squinting, he saw what looked like the head of a camel poke above the water. A creature, unlike anything he had ever seen before, surfaced, swimming along as if it owned the place. The creature's body appeared to be long and skinny, with humps and a spiny fin that peeked out of the water.

He looked around the beach as if trying to manifest another soul to validate what he saw. But he'd come to the beach alone; no one else was around. All he could do was watch the strange sea serpent swim away, until it was out of sight.

The tall tales he'd heard some of the other men share came rushing to the forefront of his mind. He remembered the locals discussing a legendary sea monster that people had reported seeing for decades. It supposedly roamed the Pacific Coast from Puget Sound, up along Canada, and on to Alaska. He always assumed the stories were invented by men seeking attention after too much whiskey and a long day of physical labor. But maybe there was more to it than that.

After several minutes, Gino walked back to the trail, away from the beach. He was certain about what he had seen, but he wasn't sure anyone would believe it.

* * *

Petroglyphs made by the Native Americans who inhabited the islands and the land around the Salish Sea depict a dragon-like creature. Reports from early settlers going back to the 1800s talk about seeing a water monster with a long, snake-like neck swimming in the area.

Reported sightings in 1933 made it into Canadian newspapers and described a "long, dark-green creature as large as a whale" in Cadboro Bay. The creature was named "Cadborosaurus" and called "Caddy" for short, a nickname given to it by journalist Archie Wells.

In 1937, a sperm whale was caught near a whaling station in Naden Harbor. When the belly of the whale was cut open, the whalers—who had seen all kinds of sea creatures—found something inside they could not identify. It was more than 10 feet long and had a head like a dog, facial features that resembled a camel, and a tail like a horse. Photos recorded the evidence, but the carcass disappeared. No one was ever able to identify what it was.

Sightings of Caddy continue to this day.

Pend Orielle Paddler

Bayview, Idaho
Fall 1944

George straightened his sailor hat and gazed out at the lake, appreciating the rare moment of silence and the chance to be alone. As a naval recruit who was training for a likely submarine assignment in the Mediterranean Sea or South Pacific, he understood that soon he would rarely be alone.

Despite its location hundreds of miles from any ocean, the Farragut Naval Training Station at the southern point of Lake Pend Oreille was an ideal training facility. The lake was one of the largest in the state and one of the deepest in the country. In the greatest depths of the lake, temperatures matched those of the ocean, making it ideal for submarine tests.

"Hey there, Georgie, what are you doing?"

George cringed at the sight of his bunkmate, Alfred. Not only was his moment of solitude short-lived, but only his mother was allowed to call him Georgie. He let it pass. "I'm just sitting and looking."

George, along with Alfred and 100 other naval recruits, had been assigned to Farragut for basic training.

"You looking for that monster you saw again?" asked Alfred.

George shrugged. "I wasn't the only one."

Alfred laughed. "But you're the only one who talks about it."

Alfred was right about that.

A few days earlier, George and five other guys were on the lake for a rowing exercise. Their rowboat was rocked by something underwater. At first, they panicked, thinking they'd accidentally navigated into the path of a rising sub. But then they saw the creature's neck and head break through the surface of the water. George had looked the thing straight in the eyes.

They tried to tell their lieutenant about it, but he encouraged them to zip their lips. George was having a hard time with that. It wasn't easy to have someone tell you that you didn't see something when you most certainly had.

* * *

May 27, 1985

Julie Green eased up on the boat's speed. She smiled at her friends, who waved back. They'd gotten out on the lake later than they'd wanted—which tended to happen when mobilizing a group of people—but they were here at Lake Pend Oreille now, and she planned to enjoy it.

"Where should we go?" she asked the group.

They shrugged.

"You're the one who knows the lake," Sarah said. "We'll let you decide."

Julie nodded. She was familiar with a substantial stretch of the lake's 111 miles of shoreline. She turned her attention back to the water and set her speed at a slow cruise. Something caught her eye.

"Look at that!" she yelled back to her friends and pointed.

A large wake appeared ahead of them, as if a boat was speeding along—except there was no boat.

As the friends tried to process what might be causing the disturbance in the water, a huge, gray creature emerged just a few hundred feet away. It swam on the surface for a moment, then dove below, the water churning behind it.

"Hold on," Julie shouted.

She increased her speed, hoping to catch whatever the thing was. She didn't come close. Soon, the wake subsided, and there was no evidence of anything out of the ordinary.

"What was that?" asked Sarah.

"Isn't there a government submarine-testing center around here?" asked their friend. "Could it have been something top secret?"

Sarah nodded. "It had to be something like that."

Julie shook her head. She was familiar with the stories of the Pend Orielle Paddler, which had been named by a local journalist in the 1970s. What she saw looked alive. It wasn't a vessel. She decided not to argue the point. It would only frighten her friends and ruin the day. But she kept a close watch on the water, just in case the creature would reappear.

"Slimy Slim" Sharlie
McCall, Idaho
Summer 1920

Hank raised the axe above his head and brought it down easily, letting gravity provide the extra force needed to cut through the wood. His crew from the Idaho Northern Railway had been tasked with cutting new railroad ties to replace the ones that had rotted, in the line that connected picturesque McCall to the rest of civilization.

He had worked in worse locations. All of Payette Lake was beautiful, but today they were near the upper point. He liked to work near the lake on a hot summer day. The air always seemed a bit cooler.

The natural body of water attracted tourists throughout the year. With the Idaho State Land Board now leasing cabins to vacationers, the railroad line had to be carefully maintained, so tourists could safely get to and from here.

Hank put down his axe and stepped back to survey the progress. Something in the water caught his attention. Looking out across the lake, he was shocked to see a stray log floating.

"Charlie, you let one get away," he shouted.

"No, boss," said Charlie. "I swear I didn't."

Hank tried to figure out how they could collect the stray log—or if it was even worth it. To his surprise, it moved back and forth, as if it had come alive and started to swim. He soon realized that he wasn't looking at a log but a creature of some kind.

Within seconds, the thing swam away fast enough to leave a trail in the water.

Hank had heard the Native American legends about an evil spirit, rumored to live within the depths of this lake. Had he just seen it?

* * *

August 1944

Loretta walked slowly along the path from her family's rented home, down to the lake. She loved it here and had always felt lucky that her family had been able to spend their vacations at Payette Lake for so many years. Now, she felt guilty and filled with dread. It seemed wrong to be on vacation when the world was at war. But her older brother Walter had insisted that the family spend his 18th birthday at Payette Lake because, after they got back, he was bound and determined to enlist and do his duty.

Thankfully, the family had finally received word (in the form of a letter) that her eldest brother, John, had survived the D-Day invasion at Normandy on June 6. Loretta's friend Margaret hadn't been so lucky; her brother would not be coming home.

Her thoughts were interrupted by loud shouts. Several groups of people stood on the beach, all pointing at the water. She hurried along to where her family was sitting.

"Look," shouted Walter. "There it is again!"

Loretta saw a water creature moving parallel to the shore. It was about the length of two cars. Its head rose up, and it looked exactly how she imagined prehistoric dinosaurs would have looked. The dark-gray humps of its back went up and down through the water.

It turned toward the shore and opened its mouth to breathe or show off—or maybe threaten the onlookers; she couldn't be sure. It had a fierce jaw and sharp teeth. Without warning, it turned and dove underwater. The spectators waited for several minutes, but they didn't see it again.

"What do you think of that?" asked Walter.

"I think it means you shouldn't go to war," said Loretta. "I just can't bear the thought of losing my brothers."

Walter put his arm around his younger sister. "I think it means exactly the opposite," he told her. "It means I'll survive so I can tell this tale—and so will John because we have to bring him here and show him for ourselves. Otherwise, he'll never believe it."

Loretta smiled and sank into her brother's arms. "Okay, I believe you."

* * *

In September 1946, the sea monster was again spotted near the shoreline of Payette Lake by more than a dozen people. By this time, the creature had earned the nickname "Slimy Slim." But by 1954, the editor of *The Star News* decided that the town could do better for its now-famous sea serpent. The paper announced a contest to come up with a new name.

Le Isle Hennefer Tury from Springfield, Virginia, declared in a letter that the monster should be named "Sharlie" after a common phrase used in a radio show where comedian Jack Pearle played Baron Munchausen. He would often ask, "Vas you der, Sharlie?"

From then on, the creature of Payette Lake was called Sharlie, and sightings have continued through the years. With 5,330 acres of water formed by glacier activity and with recorded depths of over 350 feet, the lake could be the home of a deep-sea creature that sometimes likes to come to the surface just to put on a show for onlookers.

The Giant Octopus
Tacoma, Washington
November 7, 1940

Leonard Coatsworth, an editor at *The News Tribune,* drove past a billboard advertising the Pacific National Bank. Its slogan read, "As secure as The Narrows Bridge." Touted as a symbol of human ingenuity, the bridge had opened just four months earlier and was the city's newest industrial landmark. The third-longest suspension bridge in the world, it stretched from Tacoma, across the Tacoma Narrows, to the Kitsap Peninsula.

Already a source of pride, the $6 million investment was quite an experience for anyone who used it. Nicknamed "Galloping Gertie," the bridge swayed and bounced by design. Crossing it was not for the faint of heart—or those prone to motion sickness. Construction workers who built the structure had regularly chewed on lemons to avoid getting seasick.

On this day, as a fierce storm raged, Leonard ventured onto the bridge. Glancing down, he noticed the whitecaps of Puget Sound raging vigorously below. He gripped the steering wheel a little more tightly. With nowhere to turn around on the narrow bridge, it was too late to retreat. The only way out was through—or, in this case, over.

The storm seemed to be testing the bridge . . . and his nerves. The bridge bounced more than it ever had before. Slowly, Leonard began to inch his car forward.

The bridge jerked viciously. Leonard's car skidded precariously to the side, and he lost control. Not wanting to stay in the car for another moment, he decided to brave the cold rain and get out. He lay his body flat on the bridge and crawled his way to safety on the other side.

Reaching a toll plaza phone, he called the newsroom at his paper and told them to send a reporter and a photographer to cover what might be the end of Galloping Gertie.

Leonard's hunch proved right. An hour later, several hundred feet of the Narrows Bridge lost its battle with the weather and collapsed, dropping into the swirling water and sinking into the treacherous tides of Puget Sound. It took with it Leonard's car and a beloved pet: his daughter's cocker spaniel.

As the *Tribune's* reporter and photographer headed back to their office, they noticed a peculiar sight. The Pacific National Bank billboard—which hours earlier had compared itself to the industrial innovative marvel, the Narrows Bridge—had been covered up with white paper.

However, that 600-foot section of steel, concrete, and cable—nestled 200 feet below the surface of an inland estuary—turned out to be good for something. The failed Galloping Gertie created an artificial reef. The collapsed bridge evolved and grew into a home for sea creatures, including monsters.

* * *

Titlow Beach, 2010

Douglass Brown couldn't believe his luck. The prettiest girl in school had agreed to go for a walk with him along the beach.

"Did you know they used to have the World Octopus Wrestling Championships right on this beach?" he asked her. He had kept that fact tucked away for a moment just like this.

"Really?" she asked. "What was that all about?"

"In the 1950s, divers would hold their breaths and swim down until they found an octopus. They'd drag it out of its den and see who could get one all the way to shore."

"Isn't that kind of mean?" she asked. "From what I've read, an octopus mostly just wants to be left alone."

"Yeah, probably," said Douglass. "I'm sure that's why it stopped. Now the octopuses have their own special protected areas."

"Do you believe there's a giant one?" she asked. "I've heard there's a monster-king octopus."

Douglass shrugged and took a chance, grabbing her hand. To his relief, she didn't pull it away.

"I dunno," he said. "Maybe?"

They stopped walking and looked out over the water. That's when he saw a long, tentacled arm reach up from the water.

"What's that?" he shouted, pointing at the arm that stretched nearly 15 feet above the surface.

"I don't know," said the girl. "I don't want to find out."

Together, they ran and didn't stop until they were several blocks away.

In the years to come, they both wondered if they'd glimpsed the octopus king, a sea monster that supposedly ruled the depths of Puget Sound.

* * *

2015

The commercial diver cut through the chunk of metal with a burning rod, a tool that was used to slice materials underwater. It wasn't long before he burned through his rod. His hand reached to the pile to grab another one, but he patted empty ground. Peering through the water, he shook his head in disbelief. He could see just a couple of rods left. He picked one of them up.

Holding it in his hand, he tried to remember how many he'd brought down with him. He should have more than three left—but maybe he miscounted or remembered wrong. It had been a hard day.

A long, tentacled arm reached out through the water, poking, exploring, obviously looking for something. A chill ran through the diver's body as he contemplated his own sanity. Slowly, the tentacles wrapped around the end of the rod and yanked. The monster plucked one of the diver's last remaining rods right out of his hand.

Too startled to move, he began to realize what had happened. He started to chuckle. He had just become the victim of a giant Pacific octopus's orchestrated prank.

The seasoned commercial diver knew all about the giant Pacific octopus. They were intelligent creatures that would cause mischief just for the fun of it. They could change color according to their mood and could grow to 100 pounds in a short period of time. He also knew that, if an octopus got startled, it might try to make itself look bigger by stretching its skin and puffing itself up. Witnessing this could frighten even the most experienced diver. Through the dive radios, he had heard grown men scream like children having a nightmare when startled by such a monstrous sight.

He had no idea what an octopus wanted with his burning rods—other than, maybe, to cause a little mischief.

The Sea Monster
of Wallowa Lake

Joseph, Oregon
Circa 1810

Wahluna stole a sideways glance at her new husband and tried not to smile as they walked together toward to the lake. She had been in love with Tlesca for as long as she could remember.

As children—long before either of them was old enough to understand the disagreements between their fathers—they had played together in the forest. Her father, the chief of the Nez Perce, and Tlesca's father, the chief of the Blackfeet, had agreed that as part of the treaty between the two nations, their children would be allowed to marry.

Tlesca had managed to convince them, and he had risked everything to do so. He had risked his father's approval and potential excommunication by suggesting the idea. Then he had risked his own life by coming to speak with her father. Wahluna knew that her husband was very brave and very smart.

Her father warned her that a lot of responsibility now rested on her shoulders, but she was ready. The love that she and Tlesca shared would carry them through whatever was to come.

They reached their canoe, a gift from the Kiyouses tribe that came to witness the ceremony and celebrate the promise for peace. The Yakimas tribe had come too. Wahluna wondered if she had ever seen so many people together before in her life.

With ease, Tlesca lifted the canoe onto his shoulders and carried it to the shore. Wahluna followed silently behind. She couldn't wait until they were in their boat and away from shore. She was anxious to speak freely and tell him all the things her heart was bursting to say.

He glanced back at her and smiled. Wahluna could feel that her husband was as impatient as she was for their first moment alone.

Tlesca slid the canoe into the water and put his foot inside to hold it. He offered her his hand, and she let him help her into the front. Once she was settled and balanced, he climbed in and pushed the canoe away from shore with the oar.

Slowly, he stroked the paddle to one side, then the other. Even though Wahluna wanted to turn around to watch him, she kept her eyes fixed straight ahead. She knew how important it was to show all of those watching that she had self-control.

"I am going to paddle as slow as I can, so I can be alone with you for as long as possible," he whispered.

She fought the urge to turn around and show him the smile that beamed across her face. "I thought that might be what you're doing," she whispered back. "I think you are still going too fast."

He chuckled softly.

The lake was long in one direction but short in the other. They reached the middle too soon for Wahluna. At least she wouldn't have to sit facing straight ahead anymore. They were supposed to sit together now, so they could see all of their people and those of the other nations who had come together to celebrate the treaty and their wedding.

* * *

The chief of the Blackfeet shifted his weight uncomfortably. It didn't matter that the two tribes had reached an agreement of peace. It still made him feel awkward to stand next to a man who had been his enemy for so long. But he had vowed to try; it was important to their survival. He had dreamed for many moons about how their differences wouldn't matter in the face of the evil to come. He wasn't sure what form the evil would take. He just knew that something was coming. The tribes would need to work together if they had any hope of overcoming it.

He sensed that the chief of the Nez Pierce was just as uneasy. He tried to think of something to say that would break the tension between them, but no words came to him. It would be up to their children to save them all.

He raised a hand to shield his eyes from the setting sun. Even from here, the chief could see his son's bright smile as he turned with his bride to face the crowd.

Their happiness filled him with a hope that he had not known for a long time.

He was proud of his son for finding the courage to orchestrate the agreement. From what his son told him, his new bride was just as brave. She was willing to step forward for the greater good of making peace. The chief let a smile grow across his own face—but his happiness would be short-lived.

The still lake exploded. The canoe flew into the air, tossing its occupants into the water. A giant creature with a long neck burst out of the water and thrashed its body back down, sending a huge wave of water rushing toward shore. Chaos erupted as everyone tried to comprehend what was happening.

The chief watched in horror as the scene before him unfolded. Not only had the new couple been flung from the boat, but the giant creature ate them as well.

Screams filled the air, and children cried in terror. The chief could hear his wife's wails of grief, rising above the rest.

Filled with dread, he turned to his people. "The Great Spirit is angry that we joined together. We must go. There is no longer a treaty." He led his people away from the Nez Perce camp.

* * *

November 1885

The prospector pulled on the oars, keeping them steady to propel his boat on a straight path forward. The sun was setting behind him, and he was looking forward to a fire and a hot meal.

The day had been a disappointment, but most of them were. He was sure that his hard work, patience, and persistence would pay off eventually. He just hoped it would be sooner than later. He thought about Henry, who had found paydirt in the very spot he'd been sifting just a few days prior. The prospector could feel his blood start to boil and tried to think of something else. He focused on the sound of the oars slapping in and out of the water. Its rhythm soothed his temper.

After a few minutes, he realized there was more than the sound of his own oars splashing in the water. The noise was out of sync with his rowing. He stopped to take in his surroundings. A loud splash startled him, nearly causing him to topple out of his boat. A creature with a long neck surfaced with a kick. Throwing its head about, it splashed back down, sending water in every direction.

After a moment of frozen panic, the prospector breathed a sigh of relief that the creature was gone. He set about rowing again. This time, his arms moved as fast as he could manage.

It wasn't long before he was interrupted again, this time on the other side of his boat. The creature swam nearby for a few minutes, as if showing off its size. It was nearly 80 feet long, its neck alone about 10 feet in length.

Thankfully, the man made it across the lake without being toppled over. But through the night, he tossed and turned, trying to make sense of what he'd seen. He wondered what—if anything—he should tell other people.

He decided that he wasn't going to say anything, but the next time he was in town, he couldn't help himself.

When the *Wallowa Chieftain* newspaper asked him to recount the story, he did. But he refused to let them print his name. It was one thing to talk about the ordeal in person; it was another matter altogether to think about strangers reading his name associated with a story such as this. Without knowing him personally, they'd think he was lying.

That's what he would have thought, too, if not for his personal encounter with the sea monster of Wallowa Lake. He would never forget the horror of those moments in time. His terror was real . . . so the sea monster had to be.

Amhuluk

Forked Mountain, Oregon
Circa 1700

The Kalapuya man glanced at the sun. His children had gone to the lake to dig for *adsadsh-roots*. They were supposed to return hours ago. He was worried. They were never late.

He went into his tepee and returned with an obsidian arrow tip. He sat down to wait and worked to fasten the shiny black rock as the point to a new spear. He hoped he wouldn't need it, but the work kept his hands busy and his mind from worrying, at least for the moment.

The sun was sinking when he heard his eldest son's cries carried in the wind. He hurried to meet him.

"Where are your brother and sister?" the man shouted with concern.

"It was a monster. They're gone."

His son collapsed into his arms. The man carried the boy to his bed and put him down. His body was covered in sores and rashes.

The boy's mother hurried in behind them. Silently, she began to nurse her son's wounds.

"This monster," said the man, "tell me. What was it?"

The boy winced in pain as his mother dabbed a salve on his legs. "It was . . . majestic, at first," he explained. "Its body had hair but not its legs. Its horns—they were beautiful."

"What happened?" asked the man.

The boy swallowed hard, clearly not wanting to continue. "I said how good the horns would be for us to use as tools, that we should take them and bring them home. They would help us dig deeper than we'd ever been able to dig."

The man sighed.

"And then it came at us. It glided through the mud with ease. Before we knew what was happening, it attacked. The horns, it stabbed them through my brother and sister. I ran, but it didn't chase me. It took them into the lake."

"Shhh," whispered his devastated mother. "That's enough now."

The man left the boy to rest. His wife followed him out.

"I will go," he said, picking up his spear.

The woman nodded. The look in her eyes pleaded with him to be careful, but she knew from experience that she wouldn't be able to stop him from going.

The man used the last of the daylight to follow his son's tracks to the lake at Forked Mountain. When he arrived, the water was so still that the reflected trees looked upside down, drowning in it.

The ground was soft; a bog was not an ideal place to stay. Yet he could not bring himself to leave. He set up his camp for the night and waited by the water.

In the morning, he watched the fog roll across the top of the lake, an eerie mist that seemed to have secrets to tell. Staring at the mist, the man thought about his two lost children.

Their images appeared, rising from the water. "*Didei, didei, didei,*" they said in unison.

He knew what the words meant: "We have changed our bodies."

The man wailed, unable to suppress his grief.

For five days, he stayed at the side of the lake. Over the next four mornings, his dead children came to him, saying the same words, showing their father how they had been impaled. After being visited five times, the man knew it was time to leave.

He returned to his wife and oldest child. "Amhuluk has them. The monster finds great joy in taking living things and drowning them, forcing them to stay with him forever."

Bibliography

PREFACE

Bobbe, Sarah. "A New Discovery in Alaska: The Frilled Giant Pacific Octopus." *Ocean Conservancy* (oceanconservancy.org). January 17, 2018.

No author. "Help Save the Endangered Pacific Northwest Tree Octopus." Zapato Productions intradimensional (zapatopi.net). Accessed on July 6, 2024.

No author. "Web Archives: Save the Pacific Northwest Tree Octopus." Library of Congress (loc.gov). Accessed on July 6, 2024.

BIGFOOT OF THE CASCADES
(Cascade Mountains, OR)

No author. "News Release: Sasquatch caught on camera roaming through restored natural area." City of Portland, Oregon (Portland.gov). April 1, 2022.

"The Poltergeist / Watched in the Wilderness." *Paranormal Witness* (Season1: Episode 3). September 21, 2011.

Sherrod, David. "Cascade Mountain Range in Oregon." *The Oregon Encyclopedia* (oregonencyclopedia.org). Accessed on May 26, 2024.

Staff Writer. "Bigfoot believers swap stories at convention." *Albany Democrat-Herald* (democratherald.com). May 14, 2022.

Vigliotta, Cameron. "I Camped Out Along Oregon's Bigfoot Highway, Hoping to See Something I Wasn't Sure Was There." *Willamette Week* (wweek.com). July 30, 2019.

COLVILLE SASQUATCH *(Colville, WA)*

Staff Writer. "Does Bigfoot Roam Area Near Colville?" *The Daily Chronicle.* February 17, 1971.

Staff Writer. "Footprints Add to Tale of Giant Creature Living in Washington." *Idaho State Journal.* February 17, 1971.

Vacchiano, Andrea. "Washington sheriff receives bizarre Sasquatch call from curious hunter." *New York Post* (nypost.com). March 27, 2024.

APE CANYON BIGFOOT
(Mount St. Helens, WA)

Gendron, Jared. "Tacoma deemed hot-spot for Bigfoot sightings in WA. A law protects hunters from killing it." *The News Tribune* (thenewstribune.com). May 19, 2023.

Perry, Douglas. "How a 1924 Bigfoot battle on Mt. St. Helens helped launch a legend: Throwback Thursday." *The Oregonian* (oregonlive.com). January 25, 2018.

Tulloch, Anthony. "Bigfoot Reports & Sightings in Washington State." ArcGIS StoryMaps (storymaps.arcgis.com). June 1, 2021.

IDAHO BIGFOOT *(Potlatch, ID)*

Dunn, Rick. "Bigfoot Sighting in Idaho." *Listen Boise* (listenboise.com). February 18, 2024.

Erdman, Shelby Lin. "Idaho woman blames car crash on deer-chasing Bigfoot." *The Atlanta Journal-Constitution* (ajc.com). March 26, 2017.

Satelliteinternet.com. (note: I know it's weird, but that's the byline). "Idaho is one of the states with the most per capita Bigfoot Sightings." *Idaho State Journal* (idahostatejournal.com). July 21, 2020.

BATSQUATCH *(Mount St. Helens, WA)*

No Author. "Bigfoot and Batsquatch: Find Washington's Mysterious Creatures on These Trails." *Washington Trails Association* (wta.org). Accessed on April 19, 2024.

Robers, C.R. "Mount Rainier-area youth has close encounter in the foothills." *The News Tribune.* April 24, 1994.

THE GUMBEROO *(Kingston, WA)*

Cox, T. "The Gumberoo." *Fearsome Creatures of the Lumberwoods.* Judd & Detweiler, Inc. (1910).

DeMay, Daniel, "Northwest logging scenes from the early days." *Seattle Post-Intelligencer* (seattlepi.com). January 21, 2016.

Johnson, Steve. "Monster of the Week: The Gumberoo." *The Death Cookie* (deathcookie.com). Accessed on May 26, 2024.

No author. "Life in a Logging Camp." Heronswood Garden (heronswoodgarden.org). Accessed on May 27, 2024.

FLIX, THE CONSER LAKE MONSTER *(Millersburg, OR)*

Long, Greg. "The Monster of Conser Lake." OregonBigfoot.com (oregonbigfoot.com). October 1, 1996.

Odegard, Kyle. "Millersburg's creature feature." *Corvallis Gazette-Times*. October 28, 2022.

Staff Writer. "Teenagers Sight 'Ghostly' Figure." *Albany Democrat-Herald*. July 27, 1960.

DOGMAN *(Twin Falls, ID)*

Chat with eyewitness Chuy [last name anonymous]. June 9, 2024.

"Dogman Encounters Episode 342 (A Werewolf Followed Me Home!)." Dogman Encounters (youtube.com). January 29, 2021.

No author. "One Day in Twin Falls, Idaho: How-To Maximize Your Time." Visit Southern Idaho (visitsouthidaho.com). Accessed on May 9, 2024.

WENDIGO *(Ashton and Pine Basin, ID)*

Chat with witness Andrew [last name anonymous). June 30, 2024.

No Author. "Warm River Campground." USDA Forest Service (fs.usda.gov). Accessed on June 30, 2024

Ocker, J.W. "Beware the Wendigo, the Frost-bitten Flesheater of North America's Chilly Heartland." Atlas Obscura (atlasobscura.com). October 12, 2022.

"Wendigo Encounter at Pine Basin, Idaho" *Phantoms and Monsters: Pulse of the Paranormal* (phanotomsandmonsters.com). August 12, 2019.

THE BASKET OGRESS *(Seattle, WA)*

"Dzunukwa." Storyhive (youtube.com). September 23, 2019.

"Dzunukwa: Wild Woman of the Woods." Indigenous Tourism BC (youtube.com). April 19, 2010.

No author. "Thom Hess Collection." University of Washington (guides.lib.uq.edu). Accessed on June 30, 2024.

No author. "We are the Upper Skagit Indian Tribe." Upper Skagit Indian Tribe (upperskagittribe-nsn .gov). Accessed on June 30, 2024.

Yoder, Janet. "Hilbert, Vi (1918-2008)." History Link (historylink.org). November 29, 2004.

THE WAMPUS CAT *(Clark Fork, ID)*

Alvord, Rick. "A guy can learn a lot in 113 days in the Lake City." The Coeur d'Alene Press. May 26, 1988.

Bowie, Desiree. "The Wampus Cat Myth Explained: Origins and Sightings." How Stuff Works (scientce.howstuffowrks.com). Accessed on June 30, 2024.

Newbern, Pam. "Clark Fork is home to Wampus Cat." *Bonner County Daily Bee*. Wednesday, April 13, 1988.

No author. "Legend of the Wampus Cat." *Bonner County Daily Bee*. Wednesday, March 7, 1973.

No author. "Wampus Cats Run Rampant in Idaho Forest This Spring." *The Idaho Statesman*. June 2, 1933.

BAXBAKWALANUXSIWAE *(Port Angeles, WA)*

No author, "A Book of Creatures: Baxbakwalanuxsiwae." A Book of Creatures (ABookOfCreatures.com). Accessed on June 30, 2024.

No author. "Camp Hayden." Atlas Obscura (atlasobscura.com). Accessed on June 30, 2024.

No author, "Monsters of the Pacific Northwest," Attercap.Net (attercap.net). October 5, 2020.

No author, "Striped Peak." Washington Trails Association (wta.org). Accessed on June 30, 2024.

LAKE CHELAN DRAGON *(the coast of WA)*

Dr. Harper, Elizabeth. *The Legendary Lake Chelan Dragon,* Hangar 1 Publishing (hangar1publishing.com).

Hackenmiller, Tom. *Ladies of the Lake: Tales of Transportation, Tragedy and Triumph on Lake Chelan,* Point Publishing, 1998.

No author. "The Lake Chelan Dragon." Phantoms & Monsters: Pulse of the Paranormal (phantomsandmonsters.com). June 10, 2014.

Renggli, Matt. "Legend of The Dragon of Lake Chelan." Mountain View Lodge & Resort (mlvreort.com). September 1, 2020.

COLOSSAL CLAUDE *(Seattle, WA)*

John, Finn J.D. "Offbeat Oregon: 'Colossal Claude, the great Columbia Bar Sea Serpent.'" *Lincoln County Leader* (thenewsguard.com). February 4, 2020.

Perry, Douglas. "Oregon's most famous mythical creature? It might not be the beast you think it is." *The Oregonian: Oregon Live* (oregonlive.com). March 29, 2019.

Staff Writer. "Sea Serpent of Columbia." *The Capital Journal.* March 16, 1934.

DEVIL'S LAKE MONSTER *(Lincoln City, OR)*

Litfin, Richard A. "At Last Devil's Lake Has a Monster; Delakers Tether Carcass for Good Look." *The Eugene Register-Guard.* March 5, 1950.

No author. "Devil's Lake Monster." Cryptid Wiki (cryptidz.fandom.com). Accessed on June 20, 2024.

No author. Devil's Lake State Recreation Area (stateparks.oregon.gov). Accessed on June 20, 2024.

No author. "Ghostly Encounters." Explore Lincoln City (explorelincolncity.com). Accessed on June 20, 2024.

Ruud, Cassie. "Lurking in the Deep: The Legend of Devils Lake." *Lincoln County Leader* (thenewsguard.com). June 14, 2018.

SWAN VALLEY MONSTER *(Swan Valley, ID)*

"Chasing the Swan Valley Monster." Howler Brothers (youtube.com). May 10, 2024.

Fisher, Vardis (State Director). *American Guide Series: Idaho Lore.* The Caxton Printers, Ltd. Caldwell, Idaho. 1939.

No author. "Swan Valley Monster." Cryptid Wiki (cryptidz.fandom.com). Accessed on June 22, 2024.

CADBOROSAURUS–"CADDY"
(Oak Harbor, WA)

Brenner, Kelly. "Folklore & Nature: Cadborosaurus." Folklore & Nature (metrofieldguide.com). October 23, 2019.

Ladwig, Samantha. "Meet Caddy: The Loch Ness Monster of the Pacific Coast." Culture Trip (theculturetrip.com). August 21, 2018.

No author. "A Cascadia Marine Trail Site History…" Bowman Bay, Deception Pass State Park. (wwta.org). Accessed on July 1, 2024.

No Author. "Caddy." Encyclopedia of Cryptozoology (cryptidarchives.fandom.com). Accessed on July 1, 2024.

Web, Ebeys. "History of Deception Pass Bridge." Whidbey and Camano Islands (whidbeycamanoislands.com). August 15, 2015.

PEND ORIELLE PADDLER *(Bayview, ID)*

No author. "Lake Pend Oreille's Not So Secret Submarine Base." Out There Outdoors (outthereoutdoors.com). August 27, 2023.

Patrick, Sholeh. "Meet Your N. Idaho Lake Monster," *Coeur d'Alene/Post Falls Press* (cdapress.com). September 17, 2019.

Pierce, Darby. "Farragut Naval Training Station." Intermountain Histories (intermountainhistories. org). Accessed on July 1, 2024.

"SLIMY SLIM" SHARLIE *(McCall, ID)*

Erickson, Courtnie. "The Legend Of This Lake Monster in Idaho May Send Chills Down Your Spine." Only In Your State (onlyinyourstate.com). January 12, 2022.

No author. "Sharlie: The Mysterious Monster of Payette Lake." North American Cryptids (northamericancryptids.com). Accessed on June 16, 2024.

No author. "Sharlie the Payette Lake Monster." Visit McCall (visitMccall.org). Accessed on June 16, 2024.

THE GIANT OCTOPUS *(Tacoma, WA)*

Duchamp, Cathy. "Is there really a giant octopus under the Tacoma Narrows Bridge?" *KUOW, NPR* network (kuow.org). April 19, 2016.

Foster, Lauren. "Giant Octopus Revealed." *South Sound Magazine* (southsoundmag.com). September 25, 2015.

THE SEA MONSTER OF WALLOWA LAKE *(Joseph, OR)*

Benedict, Adam. "Cryptid Profile: Big Wally (AKA: The Wallowa Lake Monster)." The Pine Barrens Institute (pinebarrensinstitute.com). August 18, 2018.

No author. "Monster of Wallowa Lake Spotted in 1885." Wallowa County Oregon Genealogy and History (oregongenealogy.com). Accessed on June 9, 2024.

No author. Wallowa Lake Monster. Cryptid Wiki (cryptidz.fandom.com). Accessed on June 9, 2024.

AMHULUK *(Forked Mountain, OR)*

No author. "A Book of Creatures: Amhuluk."
A Book of Creatures (abookofcreatures.com).
Accessed on June 8, 2024.

No author. "Amhuluk, The Monster of
the Mountain Pool." Contacting 2109
(contacting2109.com). January 11, 2018.

Skinner, Charles, M. "Storied Waters of Oregon."
Legends of America (legendsofamerica.com).
Accessed on June 8, 2024.

About Jessica Freeburg

Jessica Freeburg is an internationally published author, history nerd, and researcher of the unexplained. She has written a wide variety of books, ranging from graphic novels to paranormal fiction, as well as nonfiction focused on creepy legends and dark moments from history.

As the founder of Ghost Stories Ink, Jessica has performed paranormal investigations at reportedly haunted locations across the US. She has appeared in documentaries and shows on such networks as the Travel Channel and Amazon Prime—talking about ghosts and haunted places—and can often be heard cohosting the wildly popular podcast *Darkness Radio*.

You can learn more about Jessica's work at jessicafreeburg.com.

About Natalie Fowler

Natalie Fowler, once a practicing attorney, is now an award-winning author and ghost writer. Natalie's published works include nonfiction books on poignant—though sometimes dark—historical events and haunting legends. She is the researcher and historian for Ghost Stories Ink and has led paranormal investigations at some of the most notoriously haunted locations in the country. Inspired by the concept of spirit rescue, she cofounded a paranormal group called Paranormal Services Cooperative and has published accounts of her work as a medium in this field. You can learn more about her work and publications at nataliefowler.com.

The Story of AdventureKEEN

We are an independent nature and outdoor activity publisher. Our founding dates back more than 40 years, guided then and now by our love of being in the woods and on the water, by our passion for reading and books, and by the sense of wonder and discovery made possible by spending time recreating outdoors in beautiful places.

It is our mission to share that wonder and fun with our readers, especially with those who haven't yet experienced all the physical and mental health benefits that nature and outdoor activity can bring.

#bewellbeoutdoors